THE OPEN TOKEN ECONOMY SYSTEM

A HANDBOOK FOR A BEHAVIORAL APPROACH TO REHABILITATION

By

MICHAEL W. WELCH, M.A.

Training Specialist
Division of Special Education
Vocational Rehabilitation, Center
for Developmental and Learning Disorders
University of Alabama, Birmingham,
Alabama

and

JERRE W. GIST, M.A.

Program Coordinator
Division of Special Education
Vocational Rehabilitation, Center
for Developmental and Learning Disorders
University of Alabama, Birmingham,
Alabama

With a Foreword by:

Gerard J. Bensberg, Ph.D.

Director
Research and Training Center in Mental Retardation
Professor of Special Education and Psychology
Texas Tech University
Lubbock, Texas

CHARLES C THOMAS • PUBLISHER
Springfield • Illinois • U. S. A.

Published and Distributed Throughout the World by
CHARLES C THOMAS • PUBLISHER
Bannerstone House
301-327 East Lawrence Avenue, Springfield, Illinois, U.S.A.

© *1974, by* CHARLES C THOMAS • PUBLISHER
ISBN 398-103079-0
Library of Congress Catalog Card Number: 73 19621

Printed in the United States of America
EE-11

Library of Congress Cataloging in Publication Data

Welch, Michael W
   The open token economy system.

   1. Mentally handicapped—Rehabilitation. 2. Conditioned response. 3. Behaviorism (Psychology). I. Gist, Jerre W., joint author. II. Title. [DNLM: 1. Behavior therapy. 2. Community mental health services. 3. Conditioning, Operant. 4. Day care. 5. Mental retardation—Rehabilitation. 6. Rehabilitation, Vocational. 7. Reinforcement (Psychology) WM30 W44o 1974]
HV3004.W38   362.3   73-19621
ISBN 0-398-03079-0

TO OUR FAMILIES:

Joy and Tucke   Linda, Tracy, and Amy

FOREWORD

IT GIVES ME great pleasure to have the opportunity to write a foreword for this book. I had the good fortune of observing and, to a limited extent, participating in the development of the program described in this publication when I was Associate Director of the Center for Developmental and Learning Disorders. Although the authors had access to several good publications in the application of operant theory to the retarded as well as consultants generally knowledgeable in this area, there were many essential elements related to a comprehensive rehabilitation program which had not utilized operant theory, nor provided information about the administrative aspects of the program. Consequently, the detailed program described here is the result of many revisions which were empirically based. The authors have chosen not to dwell upon the struggles and failures which had to be dealt with before success could be achieved.

Perhaps the most impressive aspect of this book is that it does reflect a comprehensive approach to the rehabilitation of the retarded. This program provides a systematic plan for the evaluation and assessment of the retarded in vocational as well as academic and personal-social skills. Following this assessment, a plan is outlined for the establishment of short- and long-range goals for each individual client and training procedures for reaching these goals. A training sequence is suggested which begins at the functioning level of the client and moves toward the acquisition of more complex skills.

Although the criticism of programs which utilize a reinforcement approach to bring about behavioral changes is probably decreasing across the country, it is still present. The authors do deal with this problem in the book and defend its effectiveness. The arguments that it is mechanistic and removes the human relationship between instructor and client are certainly not based upon fact. Those who make such arguments generally do not understand operant theory nor have they participated in such training programs. Although a reinforcer might take the form of a token or a piece of paper which shows a point being earned for the client exhibiting a certain desirable bit of behavior, the nature of the relationship between the instructor and the client remains vital in the learning process and in bringing about positive behavior change. When an instructor sets goals for the client he is indicating that he believes in the client and the client can learn to perform the task at hand. The awarding of the token merely confirms that faith. The individualized approach followed in programmed learning requires that the instructor attend to the progress of the client and helps to communicate the message that he does care for the client and gives of himself for his welfare. In the successful programs I have observed, the relationship between instructors and clients has been warmer and more positive than in traditional classroom settings in which the instructors are teaching "the group" and giving emphasis to the tasks assigned to the class rather than the individual behavior or the class members.

Behavior modification and operant conditioning does stress the establishment of behavioral objectives. By setting individual goals on each client and maintaining performance records on his progress toward these goals, the instructor is made accountable. This approach helps to remove much of the subjective aspects of teaching and gives him daily feedback on how well his clients are progressing. It cannot but help to have reinforcing effect on the instructor because of the obvious relationship between how well he is managing the learning situation and the progress being made by the clients.

Perhaps the thing I most like about the book is the amount of material devoted to the administrative aspects of the program. Most instructional programs utilizing operant theory which fail do so because of the inconsistent responses made to the student or client by the various important persons in his life. This book not only outlines the technique of task analysis and recording client behavior, it presents a plan for achieving consistency of treatment from the various teachers, instructors and supervisors who come in contact with the individual during the day. It also describes a technique for involving the family and other individuals in the community to provide carry-over outside the school and work setting.

Because of the scope of material covered in the book, readers with limited knowledge of operant theory, mental retardation, or vocational rehabilitation might have difficulty in fully understanding certain aspects of the book or adapting the program for implementation in their own setting. However, such background material is fairly easy to find and should equip even a relatively unsophisticated reader to utilize this book to greatest advantage. This approach has demonstrated its value for a group of teen-age and young adult retardates. It is hoped that this book will not only stimulate others to incorporate these techniques with this age group but aid in the development of coordinated programs which begin at the pre-school level and gradually phase into vocationally oriented programs with older mentally retarded.

Gerard J. Bensberg

ACKNOWLEDGMENTS

THE ADMINISTRATIVE DIRECTORSHIP of the project from which this book was developed was the responsibility of Dr. Charles E. Herron. We are extremely grateful to have a boss with the administrative prowess and professional foresight to not only support but to work for a total change in rehabilitation of the mentally retarded.

The initial impetus to the development of a behavioral approach for the program described in this book was put forth by Dr. Robert P. Cantrell. His continued consultation to this project has maintained our efforts over the past three years. We must also credit the student under his direction who did so much in the initiation of the economy (Albert Finch).

We would also like to thank the Division of Psychology, under the directorship of Dr. Richard B. Allison, which not only gave us initial support but continual consultation and recommendations for program improvement.

Special appreciation is given Arthur Crotts who presently directs the operation of the economy and has put forth outstanding effort in behalf of this project.

The program could never have developed without the contribution and extra effort on the part of the staff: Mary White, Beverly Lavender, Sandra Carr, Jim Butler, Kathleen Gardner, Nancy Mazanec, Dianne Davis, Jeanne Driskill, Peggy Wood, and Eugene Sellers.

The most important contribution is always saved until last and in this case there is no exception. We would like to acknowledge and thank Janice Cox not only for her effectiveness within the program but for the patience and skill she exhibited in the preparation of this manuscript.

M. W. W.
J. W. G.

CONTENTS

THE OPEN TOKEN ECONOMY SYSTEM

A Handbook for a Behavioral
Approach to Rehabilitation

CHAPTER 1

THE COMMUNITY BASED REHABILITATION PROGRAM

T RADITIONALLY, REHABILITATION HAS modeled programs for the handicapped after similar programs for normal young adults. The major
difference in rehabilitation programs for normal young adults has been
that the demands on the handicapped have been lessened to compensate
for the handicapping condition. Additional steps are required for the handicapped to make the transition from school to work (Kirk, 1972).

EVALUATION

The consideration for disability has taken the form of diagnostic evaluation to determine areas best suited for training. The client with high scores
on an aptitude test battery in the area of mechanical aptitude might be
placed in a training program for auto repair. The client with demonstrated
verbal skills in reading and language logically should be channeled into
fields appropriate to this observed skill.

Skills to be tested are numerous, and increasing modifications of diagnostic procedures have developed. The work sample, job tryout, situational
assessment, and psychological testing have become integral parts of the
evaluation procedure for the handicapped (Sankovsky, 1969).

A work sample approach involves analyzing a particular job or part of a
job within a local industry and constructing a laboratory simulation of the
job analyzed. The work sample then is used diagnostically to determine a
client's ability to perform the job analyzed. Attempts have been made to
standardize work samples, and many are available either commercially or
through non-profit, government-supported projects.

The job tryout involves placing the handicapped person in a prearranged
on-the-job training situation in the community or in a publicly supported
vocational training program. In some cases, sheltered workshops are placement possibilities. Generally, these tryout placements are used to expose the
client to the realities of actual work and provide some indication of the
client's ability to function in supervised work activities.

The situational assessment technique has no uniformly accepted definition. It primarily consists of placing a client in a controlled, often therapeu-
tic, work atmosphere where he can be observed functioning in a variety of

situations (Dunn, 1973). The work assignments are primarily for the observation of work behavior.

The psychological testing approach primarily consists of a battery of psychometric instruments. These devices might include tests which assess intelligence, achievement, aptitude, personality and/or dexterity.

ADJUSTMENT TRAINING

Evaluation has not been the total answer to the question of what factors are required for successful employment. The handicapped continually present obstacles dissonant with the utilization of evaluation as a packaged procedure for securing employment.

Retarded clients many times exhibit what can be generally referred to as poor work habits. These clients often find more interesting endeavors than performing the task at hand. Research (House and Zeaman, 1958) has verified the fact of distractability among the retarded population. Kirk (1972) has also suggested that personal hygiene and grooming are substandard among the retarded. The adjustment to new and novel situations is also difficult for retardates (Heber, 1959). This adjustment problem is, of course, one of paramount concern at the beginning of a new job. The control of maladaptive, ritualistic, and socially inappropriate behaviors are of concern in consideration for employment. The public offender, emotionally disturbed, learning disordered, and physically handicapped also present characteristic maladaptive or restricted behaviors and physical or academic repertoires which must be controlled or somewhat accounted for before employment.

Rehabilitation's answer in handling these difficulties has been the adjustment facilities or programs. This procedure occasionally involves the teaching of academic skills, instruction in personal hygiene, and attempts to control or eliminate maladaptive behaviors. Teaching appropriate use of leisure time, money management, as well as instruction in appropriate job behaviors, is often the function of an adjustment specialist (Baker and Sawyer, 1971).

TRAINING

The standard apprenticeship training program where a student or client learns to perform the task of an auto repairman by following the example of a skilled auto repairman has become the standard for training (Saylor and Alexander, 1966). The basic assumption being purported in this traditional approach is that the subject to be taught (repairing automobiles) is the most important factor in obtaining and maintaining employment.

Possession of the skill to repair a malfunctioning automobile becomes the objective of the rehabilitation program for the client.

The above-mentioned objective has worked in the labor market for years; logically, it should work for the handicapped when consideration is given to the debilitating condition.

COUNSELING

The basic rehabilitation structure employs a counselor who accepts a case or client and contracts with a facility or program to evaluate that client's occupational potential. If capability is indicated by this evaluation, the client can then be assigned to facilities or programs on a contract basis for adjustment services and/or vocational training services.

The counselor's job becomes one of assimilating the obtained information on his client. By utilizing the program recommendations, the counselor can more accurately obtain employment for his client which best fits his client's interest, aptitudes, qualities and abilities.

PROCEDURAL CRITIQUE

Evaluation Critique

The evaluator must judge the client in every conceivable way, which, of course, would necessitate that the evaluator possess skills in the area of adjustment and training. These skills are mandatory in order to evaluate the client's potential in these areas.

The evaluation process only reports observed behavior, as does any standardized test, and can only infer future behavior (Newland, 1963); however, the client may be able to perform more complex duties if handled appropriately. The word *evaluation* implies that treatment will not take place. The evaluator has become a diagnostician and evaluation a specialized system to the rehabilitation process.

Adjustment Critique

The adjustment specialist must be familiar with evaluation techniques in order to gear his program to the client's skills. He must employ evaluation procedures in order to teach academics, personal hygiene, and behavioral change objectives to his clients.

The adjustment process, of course, cannot be performed in isolation. The major adaptation for a handicapped client has to be a change in or adjustment of inappropriate work behavior. This change can more effectively be accomplished while work behavior is being performed on an actual or simulated work activity. Research presents evidence which suggests that the

retarded child has difficulty generalizing (Robinson and Robinson, 1965).
The delinquent or the behavior-disordered has difficulty with traditional
methods or has an inability to adapt to classroom structure (Kvaraceus and
Miller, 1959). The mentally ill client performs better when overt behavior
is required of him (Ayllon and Azrin, 1968). Indications are, then, that
work behavior, as a concept, may be more adequately adjusted in a work or
work-structured activity.

Training Critique

Job training or performing a particular job is, of course, something that
a person acquires through successive stages of learning. The stages are
cumulative; that is, one step of a job learned will place this person a step
closer to successfully executing the total job. Simply stated, job training is a
learned behavior on the part of the client.

Agreement between the reader and the authors on this premise would
require then, not an auto repairman, but a person knowledgeable in demonstrated principles of learning to most effectively teach auto repair. This
premise is even further compounded when the auto repairman has to teach
a handicapped person. The auto repairman is not only deficient in principles
of learning but also in knowledge of the particular characteristics of the
handicapped population. Behaviors to be learned by the retarded population
have to be broken down into much smaller units than would be required by
a person of average intelligence (Kolstoe, 1970).

The person doing the training must also be aware of the adjustment and
evaluation information regarding the client. The trainer should employ
adjustment and evaluation techniques in order to maximize his training
effectiveness. It would be rather difficult to train a person to learn how to
remove a fan belt from an automobile if the client were more interested in
observing the mutilated bugs on the grill work. This example points clearly
to the fact that behavior control is a skill that the trainer must possess if
he is to be an effective teacher.

The trainer must be able to evaluate physical, mental and behavioral
characteristics of the client so as to more effectively meet his training
objectives. He must possess enough evaluative skill to recognize when he
is giving more information than can be assimilated by the client. The
trainer must be astute enough to know that the client's misbehavior is a
function of the client's inability to digest the information at the rate required by his instructor. The client may not possess the verbal skills
necessary to explain this problem to his supervisor. Therefore, the trainer
must be capable of observing and interpreting subtle cues, a skill which only
comes through special training.

The person training a handicapped client has to be not only a trainer, but an evaluator and adjustment specialist as well.

INTRODUCTION TO PROPOSED CHANGE

The traditional separation of roles by rehabilitation has required fragmentation of client information which has to be assimilated and analyzed by the client's counselor. This fragmentation is magnified if the client must attend different facilities to obtain the three services of evaluation, adjustment and training. It is not rare for a client to be evaluated at one facility, adjusted at the next, and trained at a third; or in name receive all three services when in fact only one has been performed. Facilities are, in many cases, located in different cities or counties of a state. These three services rendered by rehabilitation are so closely interlaced that separation is impossible; but with separation, duplication is more than just probable.

Services for the handicapped have for many years consisted primarily of the segregated handling of specific problems as they occurred. Consideration of the total functional capabilities and of the finely woven relationship between a disability and the entire physical and behavioral makeup was most often ignored.

This condition mirrored a similar isolation and fragmentation in the system of education for professionals and others who serve the handicapped. Students have received training specific to the traditional approach purported by the discipline in which they were trained. There has been no organized attempt to make awareness of related disciplines a basic part of the educational experience.

The beginning of this decade has seen a concerted national effort to redirect the education of professionals and subprofessionals to serve the developmentally disabled. Twenty-three university-affiliated facilities for the training of professional and nonprofessional personnel to work with developmentally disabled children have been established under Public Law 88–164. These federally funded approaches dictate that programs be established that are consistent with known scientific information concerning the rehabilitation or habilitation of the handicapped. These recently funded programs are not only for training of professionals, but also for research and demonstration purposes and, thereby, produce more accountable services for the handicapped individual.

Few rehabilitation or job training programs have adopted the type of service program which is empirical in nature, accountable in philosophy, and predictable in service outcome. Job training programs for handicapped individuals have generally not adopted the vast amount of favorable research information in support of a behavioral approach to learning. The experimental analysis of behavior is most adaptable to the handicapped population (Santogross, *et al.,* 1973; Dalton, *et al.,* 1973; Ingham and Andrews, 1973). Publications with direct application to rehabilitation are now available. The *Journal of Applied Behavior Analysis* and the *Journal of Experimental Analysis of Behavior* are two examples. Research from these publications is presently being applied to special education, psychology, and institutions for the handicapped, but rarely to the community-based rehabilitation process.

The data on motivation and behavior control of the handicapped emphasizes the practicality of operant conditioning and behavior management techniques within the vocational rehabilitation and vocational education structure (Phillips, *et al.,* 1971; Boren, *et al.,* 1970). The retarded can be more practically taught to read with the use of programmed reading material (Birnbrauer, *et al.,* 1965). The behavior disordered's maladaptive behavior can be more effectively controlled and changed by the use of operant conditioning methods (Zimmerman and Zimmerman, 1965). The mentally ill can reflect vast improvements in socially accepted behaviors by the utilization of a token economy (Ayllon and Azrin, 1968).

The reluctance to adopt a behavioral program philosophy has been due to the single subject design of most operant research. This design has been utilized in isolated cases by all the behavioral sciences. The lack of total program adoption has been due to the lack of information on group applications of conditioning techniques. Recent years have seen increased use of the operant paradigm within institutions for the handicapped (Schaefer and Martin, 1969; Ayllon and Azrin, 1968; Kazdin and Bootzin, 1972). This use has been on a program and administrative philosophy change basis which has been quite a variation from the isolated case usage of behavior management techniques. However, an institution has complete twenty-four hour control of a patient or client; and a community based program lacks the use of very strong primary reinforcers such as sleep, food, and personal comfort.

Community based programs have begun to develop with some degree of success (Kazdin and Bootzin, 1972). Research (Thomson, 1955) has demonstrated that behavior can be manipulated by environmental experiences. Empirically, we can agree that people generally perform according to expectancies of the situation. The crowd yells and screams at a football game, but the same crowd would not make an utterance in a chapel. Szasz (1960) has inferred that, to some degree, semantics control the way we react to people. People with "problems in living" when referred to as mentally ill are treated as physically ill. The indication is that the word *ill* connotes a particular set of behaviors or reactions on the part of others (Szasz, 1961). The consternation of many classroom teachers over the fact that a literal *hellion* in her class is the epitome of virtue in another teacher's class is evidence that control can be superimposed on behavior in one situation without regard to the total existence of the person.

A rehabilitation program as a functional member of the behavioral sciences should operate on the premise that behavior is lawful and predictable as demonstrated by Ayllon and Azrin (1968). Under this basic paradigm both research and service can be combined to produce and demonstrate that job placement and job satisfaction are predictable variables and that unacceptable or inappropriate job related behaviors can be modified to closely approximate behaviors exhibited by successfully employed individuals.

Subsequent chapters of this book will outline a behavioral approach to the rehabilitation of mentally retarded young adults. The program is applicable to all handicapping conditions; however, this book will reflect a three-year project developed at the Center for Developmental and Learning Disorders, University of Alabama in Birmingham, which is primarily directed to the rehabilitation of mentally retarded young adults. The three-year project will offer a data-based application of a behavioral approach to rehabilitation in the form of an open token economy. The word *open* implies that the program is community based and that the observed effectiveness of the program reflects client contact for only six hours per day.

The program has demonstrated a much more workable and empirical approach to obtaining the goal of vocational competence for the handicapped young adult. The program has combined the process of evaluation, adjustment and training into a single procedure. The open token economy has removed, to a large degree, subjectivity in the process of rehabilitation. The research project has demonstrated that motivation which has for years haunted the vocational educator can, to a large degree, be not only controlled, but made an integral part of the entire vocational process.

The most important change the authors are purporting is a philosophic program change to a scientifically based and empirically maintained vocational rehabilitation or vocational education procedure for handicapped young adults.

CHAPTER 2

ESTABLISHING AN OPEN TOKEN ECONOMY

R ESEARCH INFORMATION ON the application of operant conditioning programs for the handicapped (Kazdin and Bootzin, 1972) is becoming increasingly available. Programs for the control of a subject's behavior within a group setting are becoming more apparent in the literature and generally take the form of the token economy (Ayllon and Azrin, 1968; Schafer and Martin, 1969; Kazdin and Bootzin, 1972). The majority of these data are for institutional programs which have control of all reinforcing stimuli for every member of the institutional population.

The assumption is that if single subject designs work for subjects outside the institution, then these controls should work for groups of subjects. Numerous classroom management techniques have worked in the classroom with control of only available reinforcers (Dalton, *et al.*, 1973; Homme, 1969; Buckley and Walker, 1970; Birnbrauer, *et al.*, 1968).

The operant conditioning paradigm has demonstrated effectiveness in the institution, with a single subject design or a group design. These designs have shown effectiveness within the community with a single subject design but with limited data on group designs. However, with the increased information available through the utilization of classroom management, it seems more than just apparent that a vocationally designed, community based, operant conditioning program can be effectively operated.

The availability of this amount of information which demonstrated the workability of the token economy system as a motivation tool precipitated a philosophic commitment toward a behavioral approach to rehabilitation. The behavioral approach would not only be utilized on a motivational basis but on a parsimonious, scientific basis as well. That is, the rehabilitation process could be broken down or condensed into a single unit or function which would combine previously separate functions of this process. The Law of Parsimony or Ockham's Razor simply implies that you do not need a razor to cut butter. The establishment of the approach advocated by the authors would reduce an elaborate mechanism (razor) for rehabilitation to an approach which is much more concise and pragmatic. A costly, commercially produced evaluation system may represent a method for evaluation or occupational exploration. However, if the same information can be obtained and retained on a standard sheet of paper, which approach would be the more parsimonious?

Adjustment training via a psychoanalytic approach, which may take considerable time and expense, may solve the adjustment problem, but would a pragmatic behavioral application to the problem suffice? Training a retarded person to tie his shoe or change an automobile tire by the lecture method of instruction would be much less practical than using a backward fading of the chain procedure, which is a basic part of programmed instruction (Taber, Glaser and Schaefer, 1965).

The open token economy system is not only more parsimonious but more objective and lends itself to be more predictable of subject outcomes. The fact that daily information or data are collected on each subject and the fact that this information can predict performance on job related behaviors is another advocation of a behavioral approach to the process of rehabilitation. The above is also a marked change in the traditional procedure for job placement.

The collected data make the open token economy system much more accountable for its actions. That is, an approach that does not use a data orientation cannot know what effect it has had on the rehabilitation of a client enrolled in the program. Failure to rehabilitate a client can be explained away as being the fault of the subject. Under a behavioral approach, success and failure of a subject is the credit and fault of the program and staff operation of the program; not the fault of the client. The process advocated here places accountability where it should be: on the program.

The above outlined attributes of the behavioral philosophy are numerous. However, the most advantageous point is most often overlooked, that is, scientific empiricism. Empirical science makes its proof through observation of overt tangibles. The benefits and practicality of this mode of scientific thought for the behavioral sciences are numerous. First, this procedure is in the real world and is at hand. That is, no theoretical model, which may or may not coincide with the subject in study, has to be superimposed in order to have demonstrated proof. Procedures, practices, treatments, etc. no longer have to coincide with a symbolic world or second order systems which will denote order to your treatment according to the confines or limits of the theoretical model being used. For example, the use of analysis of variance (Fisher, 1948) as a proof model would dictate treatment of subjects in a particular way outlined by that model. The analysis of variance model would only tell you, then, whether your treatment produced the observed change significantly greater than chance would produce the change. The utilization of the findings is restricted only to the population in the original test, with limited generalization. A behavioral approach deals only with increased and decreased frequencies of occurrence of behavior which has been defined according to the operations involved.

The above discussion outlines the philosophy of the open token economy. The program discussed is operated and maintained on the above-mentioned premises in order to maximize its effectiveness.

STAFF TRAINING

Training of staff to operate a program which employs operant conditioning techniques is an arduous undertaking. Baseline periods taken on token economies indicate that supervisors, instructors, teachers and others often maintain and increase the frequency of occurrence of inappropriate responses by positively reinforcing maladaptive behaviors. However, the importance of such training for supervisors of handicapped populations is attested to by numerous training manuals (Bensberg, 1965, 1966; Homme, Csanyi, Gonzales and Rechs, 1969; Patterson and Gullion, 1968; Gist and Welch, 1972; Atthowe, 1967).

These data reflect the difficulty and importance of having and maintaining an adequately trained staff in operant conditioning procedures. There is some indication that a program can be operated with minimal staff training (Kuypers, *et al.*, 1968; Meichenbaum, Bowers and Ross, 1968). However, a recent review of token economy programs and procedures indicates the desirability of a highly trained staff (Kazdin and Bootzin, 1972).

OPEN TOKEN ECONOMY PROCEDURES

The procedures for staff training under the open token economy consisted of six months of preparation and planning. All staff members were required to do outside reading with one abstract of the required material written per week. Training materials included journals, books, films, and programmed instruction materials related to the utilization of operant conditioning methods.

In-service training sessions were conducted weekly during a three-month period prior to initiating any treatment procedure. The data, theory and application of information from classical conditioning, operant conditioning, and modeling procedures were presented by the use of lecture, overhead transparencies, slides, and motion pictures. The staff was required to rate procedures of classroom teachers, via video tape, according to his handling of maladaptive behaviors. The staff rated and discussed the teacher's performance according to its consistency with known operant conditioning principles. Staff members themselves were video-taped and received evaluative review by their peers.

A period two weeks prior to and two weeks following a trial baseline period was concerned with operant conditioning procedures and, specifically, its application to token economies and anticipated problems related to economy implementation. These training sessions were held daily for the four-week period.

Even with the extensive training outlined above, the trial baseline period was a disaster. This trial baseline period yielded 90 percent of all evaluation measures figured above the 80 percent level of proficiency which would reflect that all the subjects on the economy were ready for employment! The trial baseline was plotted and discussed for two weeks to ascertain causes of the erroneous data. The staff as a unit determined a number of difficulties which were reflected by the trial data collection.

The first problem was inappropriately written job descriptions. The job descriptions (data collection device), which should have been written as behavioral objectives, were not accurately completed according to the client's observed performance on a job. The analysis of the objectives reflected, to a large measure, that the degree of performance required by the subject was not included on the job description. Furthermore, numerous job descriptions were found to be interpreted differently by individual staff members. For example, a job description for making change for one dollar had no degree criterion. This left the supervisor to personal judgment as to criterion. It was then relatively easy to say, "Well, the subject only errored ten times out of one hundred so I will check it 'Yes.' " The next staff member to check the job description would say, "The job description does not reflect a degree, so even though the subject only errored once in five hundred attempts, I will mark it 'No.' " A continuous effort was initiated at this point to make all job descriptions error-proof, if at all possible. The job description revision to insure objectivity and accuracy became a continuous process in the light of new data.

The trial baseline reflected numerous other problems in the mechanics of operation of the token economy. The variation in time of staff wrist-watches caused distortion of punctuality data, the writing of the client's name on so many data sheets was extremely laborious, the staff waited in some cases six hours before recording the data from memory, the client's maladaptive behaviors were handled as before the baseline; but this behavior was not recorded and numerous problems were observed which contributed to the disasterous trial run. These problems were compiled into a list of basic rules for the operation of the economy which were not only issued, but were discussed on numerous occasions. A feedback mechanism was established for the staff members as to their performance on collecting, recording, and in general, carrying out the basic economy rules.

The economy rules were:

1. A punctuality, grooming, and work assignment job description will be given to each client upon reporting to his first work station. The client

will fill in his name, date, and check his own punctuality. He will be praised if on time and paid immediately for his punctuality and grooming.

2. The time recorded on the job description as time started will be the actual time the client starts on step number one of the description.

3. Each client will have in his possession the job description on which he is actively working.

4. Each client will be checked on the basis of observed performance only. If there is any doubt as to whether the performance meets criterion, it will be checked "No."

5. The client will be checked as he progresses through the assigned job description. He will be checked at least every thirty minutes. Appropriate *positive* instruction will be given at this time and his job description checked.

6. Clients will be marked "leaving the work area" unless they check with their supervisor before leaving. (Any time over five minutes away from work area automatically constitutes leaving work area.) In evaluation and adjustment work areas, random times will be selected to determine excessive talking and idleness.

7. The concept of successive approximation in assigning amount of work will be strictly adhered to.

8. Each step of the assigned job description will be checked with appropriate positive feedback to the client.

9. Each client will be paid upon completion of the assigned job. No delayed payment of clients is acceptable. It will be the responsibility of the immediate supervisor to see that the clients are paid.

10. Problem behavior will be dealt with under the confines of the token economy. If any assistance is needed, check your manual.

11. All job descriptions assigned will be *typed* on appropriate color level before being issued to clients. (If client does not have a job description, he may not perform that job.)

12. Appropriate color level assignments to clients will be adhered to according to the color hierarchy.

13. Paid and checked daily job descriptions will be filed in the daily file book no later than 2:15 P.M. each day.

14. It will be the responsibility of the administrative personnel to see that these rules are carried out.

These rules are placed here to emphasize their importance. A full understanding of these rules will become clear as the reader progresses through the subsequent chapters.

The in-service sessions were not stopped after the economy was initiated. Weekly sessions were held after the successful initiation of the economy. The practice has continued with only one change. At present, the training is being conducted by the staff members.

PROGRAM ANALYSIS

Program Objective

The consideration of instituting a motivational system raised important questions for the program. The basis seemed to be "Motivation to what end?" A study of the reasons for the program funding and reasons for the program's existence reflected one objective—employment of the handicapped person. The primary purpose of the open token economy was to place handicapped individuals on a job for which they in turn would earn a wage. Of course, placement only is not the answer to a vocational or job training program. The answer is job satisfaction or adjustment (remaining on the job), ability to perform the desired job or task (skills), economic security (self-support), and a job which fits the observed skills of the handicapped person. Placement on a job and a wage earned becomes a function of evaluation, adjustment and training. The question left unanswered is: "What are the behaviors required which will give the handicapped person job satisfaction and job stability?"

TARGET BEHAVIORS

The handicapped person is primarily employed in a service occupation which he is physically able to perform (Kirk, 1972). His inability to hold that job is not a function of his inability to physically perform, but a function of his inability to follow directions, stick to a task, his academic competencies, and his inappropriate job behaviors. These job behaviors may reflect themselves in talking and not working, daydreaming, not attending to task at hand, not being punctual because he cannot tell time, and being unable to punch the time clock. These and many other socially inappropriate behaviors are the *cause* of the handicapped individual's downfall in the job market.

The open token economy was begun with the above-mentioned problems in clear view. The program set out to identify particular behaviors which are problems to employing the handicapped. These target behaviors were sectioned into the following categories: (1) auxiliary work behaviors; (2) work behaviors; (3) academic behaviors; (4) following directions; (5) motivation; and (6) homemaking behaviors.

Under the auxiliary work behaviors specific job-related behaviors were identified which would be a function of securing and maintaining employment. The worker must be punctual. Not only will tardiness lower the amount of money earned, but the hours are established by the employer because a work need is eminent at that time. If the employee is not on the job during this time, the work must go undone. Another auxiliary work behavior is grooming. This particular behavior becomes increasingly apparent in service occupations because of contact with people. There is nothing less appetizing than a waitress with body odor. The time clock has become a standard for the employer; and its effective use is more than just apparent, and, of course, it is a behavior auxiliary to actual work.

Work behaviors were identified under the category of "Works at a Steady Pace." All of these behaviors seemed to be of a negative nature. That is, the things which connote steady work are not being idle, not leaving the work area, not talking to excess with fellow employees. These target behaviors were left with a negative connotation initially and included in the economy as *gigs* or punishments when they occurred. A solution to the punishment aspects of this approach was subsequently reached and will be discussed in subsequent chapters of this book.

Academic behaviors were also of prime importance in maintaining competitive employment. The academic level is, of course, a good yardstick to success on a job. The identification of specific academic behaviors of primary importance was the most pressing problem. Since the acquisition of academic skills is the most difficult task for the mentally retarded, improvement in basic academic skills (reading, writing, arithmetic) was stressed. This was not only the most important, but most expeditious procedure to follow for appropriate job placement.

A supplement to academic training *per se* is the utilization of a driver education, traffic safety training program. The driver training program not only ensures safe drivers, but assures that the handicapped client will be able to provide his own transportation to and from work in the absence of the transit system. Two other factors are related here: one is the cost factor in utilizing public transit; the other is a 10 percent reduction in the cost of insurance for clients who successfully complete a driver training program. Perhaps the greatest feature of this program is the new job opportunities available in the areas of delivery, cab driving, truck driving, and numerous other occupations which require the utilization of a motorized vehicle.

The next target behavior was considered one of the most basic elements of the open token economy. The confusion of the mentally retarded in following directions, understanding what particular behaviors were required for successful completion of the job, and fulfilling these requirements in a sequential order became a paramount difficulty for the mentally retarded client. A program was so structured as to develop specific goals in the form of behavioral objectives which could be realistically met by each client. These goals began as very specific step-wise directions and graduated to the completion of desired tasks through much more general directions as to specific job requirements. The clients were able to learn through a slow and progressively more difficult procedure to adequately cope with realistic job requirements.

Motivation of the handicapped population as well as the normal population is an extremely important factor in job success. The active, excited and aggressive employee who produces a salable item or provides service for which the consumer will pay is the key factor in a competitive society. The degree to which the employee produces is an empirical determinant of continued employment.

The last identified target behavior fell under the category of homemaking behaviors. These were identified as behaviors which would make the client economically useful at home. The ability to plan and prepare budgeted meals, repair tattered wearing apparel, make clothing, and, in general, do numerous household tasks which reduce the cost of living were considered as homemaking behaviors.

These general target behaviors were outlined as being the areas to be learned by clients in order to become contributing members of the economic work force. Each of these target behaviors will be discussed in detail in the following chapters which will also outline specific adaptation procedures for program application.

PROGRAM IMPLEMENTATION

The basic objectives and behaviors to be changed in order to meet those objectives were now generally outlined. The next step was the configuration of the program so as to offer proof of success in meeting the previously stated objectives. The program philosophy dictated that empirical data be collected on each subject toward a terminal goal. Data have to be recorded in such a manner as to eliminate subjectivity, standardize procedures, ensure convenience of recording, and maintain a permanent record of information from which decisions may be made as to appropriate treatment. This recording device had to be so devised to fit a single client as well as the entire program. The device also had to offer proof that behavior was being changed toward an approximation of the behaviors required for successful employment. This device was developed and called the program's *job description*.

The empirical justification of the program had to be apparent which required a utilization of an operant paradigm. This includes a period of empirical observation without treatment (baseline) and a period of treatment in which any decrease or increase in performance on the part of the clients would be noted. The treatment to be used in this particular case was a secondary reinforcer (a learned reward) which could be exchanged for a primary reinforcer (satisfaction of a particular need or desire). The secondary reinforcer was a token. A token could be exchanged by the clients for numerous positive reinforcers. Money was obtained through the present operating budget to purchase through petty cash edible rewards such as candy, crackers, gum, etc. Where at all possible, natural contingencies (things that naturally occur after a behavior is emitted) were used. Things which the clients were observed to work for that generally cost nothing were then made contingent upon appropriate work behavior. Such things as television time, utilization of the telephone, lunch, and free time were all made contingent reinforcers.

The point that should be stressed here is that the establishment of the token economy did not increase the program operating budget. The program was established and operated within the confines and limitations of the existing operating budget.

After the data were collected, an organized system of retrieval and condensation of the data had to be established. The training of staff was of paramount importance in the utilization of an operant conditioning paradigm.

A commitment was made by staff to organize and put into effect an operant conditioning token economy program for vocational rehabilitation students and clients. This commitment began in June, 1970, at which time staff training was begun. The writing of job descriptions began at the end of that month. Descriptions had to be written for all jobs that clients performed during the day. Writing and rewriting of job descriptions was completed in October. The staff began taking baseline on October 1, 1970. After one week of baseline, it was evident that the staff had not been properly trained. Baseline was discontinued because of poor data collection and what was evaluated to be biased data. The staff training continued until November 2, 1970. A two-week baseline was taken after which the token economy was initiated.

As demonstrated from this brief outline of events that took place, it took from May until mid-November to get an economy into operation. This was a six-month period of planning and preparation. At the present time, it is evident that the original economy was somewhat lacking. The system, since its inception in November, 1970, has gone through many changes. The original pilot group consisted of twenty-two subjects; data and graphs were hand-plotted. There are now seventy subjects on the economy utilizing a computer data system. Graphs are computer printed and a daily banking balance is tabulated. Metal tokens were originally used. They could be borrowed, stolen or hoarded. A paper token (like a cashier's check made out to the subject) is now used. These tokens are color coded for different areas enabling evaluation of earning and spending patterns. An economy bank has eliminated the necessity of holding large amounts of tokens for lunch and other reinforcers. Tokens can be deposited in the economy bank and checks written. The system has developed from charging tokens for absences, to the subject's earning sick leave days by attendance, to buying with tokens insurance against absence due to illness. The system has evolved from the unsophisticated dispensing of rewards by staff to reinforcement contingent upon appropriate behavior. Reinforcing contingencies have expanded and continue to expand daily. Subject responses to the reinforcement also change almost daily.

The economy, at present, is the same in theory as the one begun in 1970, but not in application. It is much more sophisticated and effective. The data taken from the present system is much more accurate and reliable. All problems have not been eliminated, and the system is changed when it does not meet the needs of the subjects. This system gives the program much needed data and recorded information about each subject on a daily basis. Before 2:15 P.M. each day all percentages, token values, and job codes are checked and filed. These data, along with the master banking sheet for the day, are keypunched and verified for the 8:15 A.M. printout the next morning. As needed for staffing, cumulative graphs are computer plotted.

This procedure is one of the first scientific approaches to job placement and rehabilitation of clients attempted in the state of Alabama. The placement of clients on jobs no longer has to be on the basis of biased personal opinion, but on the hard data collected and analyzed individually. The assumption underlying this program is that behavior is lawful and predictable. If this is true, unacceptable job behaviors can be changed to acceptable job behaviors.

CHAPTER 3

THE JOB DESCRIPTION

THE JOB DESCRIPTION is the program base or the central unit around which the program operates. The primary function of the job description is a means of recording work performance data on individual clients. The description has to be written in such a manner as to facilitate convenience on the part of the staff in recording target behaviors. It has to be easily manipulated and easily understood by all who utilize it; therefore, each description must be standardized so that all information is contained on as little space as possible and so that the client and staff member know the exact location of all relevant information needed to accurately complete the description.

BEHAVIORAL OBJECTIVES

A program has to be analyzed according to the basic job requirements within that program. For example, in order for a client to become a proficient employee in a printing office, he must know how to perform certain jobs. He must be able to operate a duplicating machine so that he gets a clear and flawless replica of the original copy. He must be able to operate an offset printing press and do all the things which are required for proper maintenance, care and utilization of this machine. The point to this discussion is the fact that any job requires numerous tasks for its successful completion. The jobs within a training or evaluation program have to be analyzed into component parts. The job of a building services employee would be composed of numerous jobs such as dust mopping, cleaning cigarette urns, cleaning stairwells, dusting, and numerous other tasks which are related to the general requirements of building services employees. The job then must be broken down into single jobs. The single job then requires many different behaviors. For example, if a client is to wet mop a corridor, he must have in his possession the supplies needed to adequately clean the surface of the floor without leaving soap residue; he must clean the floor in a figure "8" pattern so as to ensure that the entire surface of the floor is free of dirt; after completion of the job he must adequately care for his equipment.

Each specific behavior required of a client within a program must be broken down into its component elements. Each component element must then become a goal or objective to be reached by the client. This means that the task of wet mopping a floor is the entire job. The basic parts of that job can be broken down into smaller segments. These smaller segments then can become subgoals which, when combined, produce the end product of a correctly mopped floor.

An employee on a real world job will have numerous specific jobs which are combined to produce his total job requirements. The analysis of total job requirements in a retrogressive process can produce the starting point and successive stages of each specific task. The specific jobs in combination then become the completion of the total job requirements. If jobs within a program are to be analyzed to component parts, the most proficient way of doing this is to utilize behavioral objectives.

The behavioral objective is a relatively new concept which is becoming a standard in the field of education (Mager, 1962; Bloom, 1956). The basic components of a behavioral objective are listed as (1) a description of who is to learn, (2) a requirement of an observable response, (3) the setting or where the behavior is to be performed, and (4) the level of attainment or a criterion score. These objectives have to be written in behavioral terms; that is, they can only utilize words or terms which are descriptive of particular behaviors. The description of a model citizen in the American society leads to differences in agreement as to what constitutes a model citizen. Many people would characterize themselves as being model citizens; however, inspection of their behaviors may reveal a very different civic behavior pattern. In order to be empirical and communicative as to job requirements and to remove surplus meanings that are inherent in many words in the English language, objectives have to be defined in terms of the behaviors required to perform those objectives.

The above procedure would place requirements for successful completion of an objective into a visual or observation modality so that questions of success could be empirically agreed upon. Words such as *write, deliver, construct, select, order, transfer* and *distinguish* all require observable behaviors; whereas words such as *know, appreciate* and *understand* all require cognitive processes which are not observable. It would be impossible to adequately measure the following objective: The subject will be able to fathom mathematical abstractions; but would be relatively simple to observe whether or not a person could perform the next objective: The subject will write the correct answers to four of the five presented short division problems. Each objective must not only be in behavioral terms but must have a success criteria. The success criteria determines the degree of performance required for successful completion.

An objective which states the following has no degree criteria: The subject will correctly make change from a dollar. The subject was to perform the behavior of making change from a dollar but does not reflect how often or frequently this behavior is to occur. A better approach would be: The subject will successfully make change for one dollar, nine out of ten trials. This objective clearly could be observed by any number of individuals; each individual would be able to say whether or not the behavior was actually performed by the subject. Besides being adequate in measurability, the job description objectives have to be sequential in nature.

SUCCESSIVE APPROXIMATION

The removal of an automobile tire is a perfect example of the sequential nature required of behavioral objectives. Tire removal requires that the hub cap be removed, the wheel nuts loosened, the automobile jacked up, the nuts removed, and, lastly, the tire removed from the hub. The tire cannot be removed without completion of the previous steps required in the removal of the tire. However, the completion of step number one (removal of the hub cap) advances the person one step closer to the removal of the entire tire. He has not met with success for the total job, but he is successful on step number one. Program utilization of this concept also involves a more basic concept—successive approximation. The definition of this concept is a basic strategy in operant conditioning; that is, a particular behavior may be non-obtainable as an end product. However, by breaking down this end product into successive stages and positively reinforcing each stage of development, the entire process may be achieved with maximum accuracy. For example, in order to get a child to socially interact with a group, a supervisor may inform the child that interaction with the group is important, yet subsequent interaction never occurs. However, reinforcement of the stages required in order to have group interaction cannot only be achieved, but maintained by the utilization of appropriate reinforcement for appropriate behavior.

The one-step completion concept stimulates the next step and the next, the next, and so on with the end result being the achieved terminal state. Take for example a child learning to walk. While standing close to the child, attempts at taking the first step will be made in that the child is assured of security and support by the parent. However, if the parent stands some ten to twelve feet away and says, "Walk," the child will more than likely sit down or not attempt to make the effort. But the closer to the child the parent is, the more apt the child is to make the first step. Then a gradual increase in the distance between parent and child will gradually increase the motorical behavior of walking.

Successive approximation is quite akin to another concept of behavioral programming; this is the concept of *fading*. Fading is nothing more than gradually increasing the amount of behavior for the same amount of reward. The job description would require not only completion of step number one for reward, but the completion of steps number one through four for the same amount of reward. The client who is observed to successfully complete steps one through four on each job description no longer has to be paid for steps one through four but only on steps which require behaviors which have not been perfected by the client. An example of fading may be that the duplicating machine operator knows how to assemble supplies, prepare the machine, and begin duplicating, but has a great deal of difficulty in counting the number of copies. The entire job description then may be amended to include only the fact that he does not count the number of copies, thereby making all reinforcement contingent upon counting the correct number of copies. A behavior which has been well established in the repertoire of work behaviors exhibited by clients can be gradually faded off reinforcement, leaving only the behaviors that have not been obtained to be required for securing positive reinforcement.

TOKEN VALUE

Where at all possible a token value of a completed job should be assigned. The token value is noted in the top center portion of the job description below the title as in Figure 1, Section A and indicates the amount of tokens payable to a client on the successful completion of the job. The token value is instituted so as to maintain a high performance rate. If the job is paid per hour, the client could linger at a task without totally completing the job and receive the same amount of money as doing the job in a step-wise fashion and completing it in a very short period of time. The token value will then be an incentive for the client to complete the job and to go on to the next job in order to earn more tokens, whereas being paid by the one-half hour would earn the same number of tokens without actually completing the job.

Not only should the client be paid by the token value, but token value in relation to percentage of correct response. A hurriedly completed job without attention to detail will present a less accurate percentage figure than will a detailed completion of the task. The reduction in percentage also reduces the amount of tokens that can be earned and thereby lessens the amount of reinforcement. Reinforcement then is maintained to be contingent upon appropriate speedy performance of a job and inappropriate or idle behaviors are not reinforced. The percentage is calculated and explained to the client on the basis of the type of description on which the client is working. This information will be explained in Chapter 4.

Three types of jobs should be established which involve the utilization of all the concepts previously mentioned. The concept of fading, successive approximation, and appropriate use of behavioral objectives should all be included in leveling the job description. The first level of job descriptions

CENTER FOR DEVELOPMENTAL AND LEARNING DISORDERS

10/13/72   TOKEN ECONOMY

	MAIL CLERK	NAME_____
A ➤	TOKEN VALUE 4	
	TIME 30-45 MINUTES	DATE_____

YES | NO

1. REPORT TO 1st FLOOR MAIL BOXES AT 10:30 a.m. AND 2:00 p.m.

2. SORT MAIL DEPOSITED IN TRAY.
   A. SORT CAMPUS MAIL
   B. SORT MAIL WITH POSTAGE STAMPS
   C. SORT MAIL BY GRANT NUMBERS
   D. COLLECT MAIL NOT FOR CDLD
   PLACE RUBBER BANDS AROUND SORTED MAIL

8. UNLOCK MAIL BOXES NOS. 311 & 313 BY COMBINATION.

9. COLLECT MAIL FROM BOXES AND PLACE INTO BASKET.

10. RETURN TO CDLD.

11. SORT ALL MAIL INTO MAIL BOXES ON 1st FLOOR.

12. INFORM SUPERVISOR WHEN JOB IS FINISHED.

CODE _____ 185 _____
TOKENS _____
B ➤ PERCENTAGE_____%

TIME FINISHED_____

TIME STARTED_____

Figure 1. Job description indicating token value and percentage.

can be printed on blue paper. (For a complete listing of blue level jobs see Appendix A) These descriptions should include very menial tasks. The descriptions of hand sanding, cleaning the toilet, wet mopping, and the like may all be on a blue level which requires the client to perform tasks which carry no status, no socially redeeming value, and is generally done in the absence of other people. The client may receive the same amount of tokens for this job that he does for a higher job level; however, this job carries less value as far as prestige, credit, and behavioral expectations are concerned. The next level can be referred to as the green level. (See Appendix B for examples) This is one step higher than the blue level and requires more responsibility on the part of the client. More difficult behaviors, such as accuracy, neatness and responsibility, can be required for the successful completion of a green level job. The behavioral objectives written on each of the green level jobs should be less structured and require more client decision than do blue level jobs. The majority of the clients within the program function on this level rather than the low or the high level primarily because, in establishing the program, green level could be considered the median production performance level of clients enrolled in the program.

The last level of consideration can be termed the red level job. (See Appendix C) These jobs require maximum decision making, responsibility, and performance acuity. These are the jobs that will be performed on actual job placements. This level of proficiency can only be attained through successful completion of blue and green level jobs and the assurance through performance that red level jobs can be performed accurately and reliably by the client. Jobs at this level may include office courier, bus driver, teacher aide, and/or mail clerk. All of these jobs require academics, sophistication, dependability, and personal initiative. Where the successful completion of a blue level job requires a clean floor, the successful completion of a red level job might require completion of floors, cigarette urns, venetian blinds, and other cleaning behaviors in the same amount of time. The red level then becomes an end product or a combination of numerous blue and green level jobs into a total job responsibility. A red level job for teacher aide may be an explanation of ten to twelve separate jobs rolled into one description. The objectives within the red level job should be much less specific than the blue level and green level performance criteria. Red level objectives more accurately approximate what would be required on actual job placement.

The percentage of performance obtained on a blue level job is not at all equated with the percentage obtained on a red level job. The percentage is relative to the degree of performance. A client must progress from blue to green and from green to red levels. Each level requires more generalized work behaviors for approximately the same amount of reinforcement. The percentage of performance is noted at each level and theoretically should be maintained at a high degree for each level. A high percentage on blue would suggest the fading to the next highest level and the subsequent wait for improvement in this level of performance to a particular success criterion, say 85 percent, and upon attainment of this level, movement to the next level and a subsequent wait for percentage improvement there. The ultimate performance should be 90 percent to 100 percent on all red level jobs performed which would be indicative of a high probability of successful performance on any comparable job within the community.

The work behaviors are the only job descriptions which are part of the hierarchical arrangement of levels. Academic and auxiliary work job descriptions are printed on white paper and carry no significance as to color.

Academic incentives come from the progression of book levels in reading and math. The graduation from book level to book level is a periodic *pat on the back* and assurance that success is being achieved. The material being used is programmed instruction which emphasizes strongly the concepts of fading and successive approximation.

CHAPTER 4

TYPES OF JOB DESCRIPTIONS

THE JOB DESCRIPTION cannot be totally standardized by location such as workshop, homemaking, or academic areas, but must be established as closely as possible to standard format; each area format should be standard for that particular area. Four types of job descriptions should be established: work job descriptions, academic job descriptions, auxiliary work job descriptions, and the self-help descriptions. The work job description should be a definite outline of particular behaviors required for successful completion of the work job description.

CONSTRUCTION OF THE WORK JOB DESCRIPTION

Each job description should be assigned a token value. The token value becomes the total amount of tokens that can be earned for the successful performance of a particular job. However, it is sometimes difficult to estimate the amount of time required to perform a work task. Therefore, an assignment of so many tokens per half hour is required for some work job descriptions. This is or can be a temporary device to gather data over time to establish the amount of time it takes the average client to perform this work task. After these data have been collected, an appropriate token value can be assigned. The concept of assigning token values is the same concept one might utilize in having his lawn mowed. That is, the person to mow the lawn is not paid in advance nor is he paid by the hour. Payment by the hour would ensure that the person would take as long as possible to finish the task so as to earn more money. Withholding the money until the lawn is mowed successfully ensures speedy and efficient lawn mowing behavior. The same concept holds true with the token economy. The incentive, or reinforcement, should be just that. It should not reinforce dawdling and lackadaisical behavior. Therefore, the token value is an essential part of the work job description. The token value can be written directly under the job title so that the client can easily see the value of the job and an estimate of how quickly it should be done (See Figure 2, Section A).

The next major element of the job description is the job description title. The title should be written as briefly and specifically as possible using

27

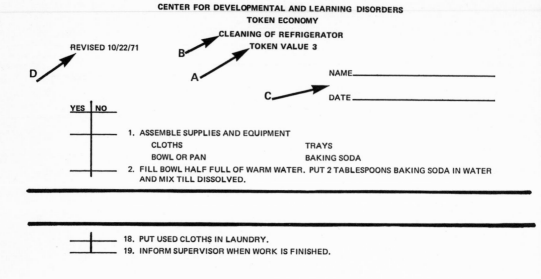

Figure 2. Sections of the job description.

simple nomenclature that is easily identified by the client (See Figure 2, Section B).

Spaces for name and date should be in the top right hand corner and should be filled out by the client with a quick check by his supervisor (See Figure 2, Section C).

The job description should be revised when necessary; each revision should carry a date so that a quick, easy identification can be made on the successive stages of development of the program economy. This date can be written just above the objectives and in plain view for comparison (See Figure 2, Section D).

The next major element of the job description is the objectives themselves. Written, of course, in terms of the behaviors required to complete the job, they are in successive stages with each stage being a task in and of itself. The steps are successive in nature with the first being a prerequisite for the second and a second a prerequisite for the third and so on. Each step requires a "yes" or "no" check by the supervisor. The client either success-

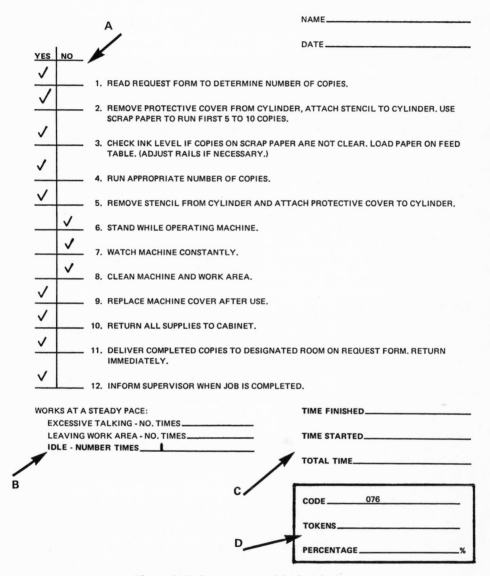

CENTER FOR DEVELOPMENTAL AND LEARNING DISORDERS
TOKEN ECONOMY
10-22-71   **DUPLICATING MACHINE OPERATOR**
TOKEN VALUE 3 PER ½ HOUR

A

NAME

DATE

YES	NO	
✓		1. READ REQUEST FORM TO DETERMINE NUMBER OF COPIES.
✓		2. REMOVE PROTECTIVE COVER FROM CYLINDER, ATTACH STENCIL TO CYLINDER. USE SCRAP PAPER TO RUN FIRST 5 TO 10 COPIES.
✓		3. CHECK INK LEVEL IF COPIES ON SCRAP PAPER ARE NOT CLEAR. LOAD PAPER ON FEED TABLE. (ADJUST RAILS IF NECESSARY.)
✓		4. RUN APPROPRIATE NUMBER OF COPIES.
✓		5. REMOVE STENCIL FROM CYLINDER AND ATTACH PROTECTIVE COVER TO CYLINDER.
	✓	6. STAND WHILE OPERATING MACHINE.
	✓	7. WATCH MACHINE CONSTANTLY.
	✓	8. CLEAN MACHINE AND WORK AREA.
✓		9. REPLACE MACHINE COVER AFTER USE.
✓		10. RETURN ALL SUPPLIES TO CABINET.
✓		11. DELIVER COMPLETED COPIES TO DESIGNATED ROOM ON REQUEST FORM. RETURN IMMEDIATELY.
✓		12. INFORM SUPERVISOR WHEN JOB IS COMPLETED.

WORKS AT A STEADY PACE:
  EXCESSIVE TALKING - NO. TIMES
  LEAVING WORK AREA - NO. TIMES
  IDLE - NUMBER TIMES

TIME FINISHED

TIME STARTED

TOTAL TIME

B

C

D

CODE   076

TOKENS

PERCENTAGE   %

Figure 3. Token economy job description.

fully completed the step or did not successfully complete the step according
to the previously outlined criteria. A correctly written objective will clearly
identify success and failure on each step with little or no judgment required
by the supervisor. The supervisor can simply check "yes" or "no" (See
Figure 3, Section A) to each item or objective and upon completion of the

job description figure a percentage of success by dividing the number of possible "yes" checks into the number of "yes" checks.

The work job description is the only type which contains a *gig* or punishment aspect. This is the "Works at a Steady Pace" section located just below the behavioral objectives. This section is added primarily because a token value cannot be assigned to all job descriptions (See Figure 3, Section B). The procedure here is to randomly set a timer in the work area and when the timer bell rings, anyone who is talking or has left the work area, or who is not actively engaged in work is given a mark in one of the three categories which is subsequently figured as a "no" check when the total percentage for the job is calculated. The timer bell is set on a random schedule so as to maximize the rate of responding by the utilization of a variable interval schedule of punishment.

Certain difficulty will result if proper precautions are not set forth for accounting for exact amounts of time reported to complete the job. If the supervisor waits until the clients under his supervision are gone to figure the amount of time, he is assured of inaccuracy and will thereby reinforce clients for idle time. A quick, easy solution to this problem is the "Time Started: Time Finished" section of the job description in the lower right hand corner of the description (See Figure 3, Section C). The location in this particular position is important in that it will allow the description to be placed inside the time clock and a time punched for starting and a time punched for finishing. If the time finished is placed above the time started, easy computation of total time worked is possible. This procedure will ensure that an accurate time estimate for each job will be calculated. This time estimate will become important data in figuring later token values and in determining a client's progress on replication of these job behaviors.

The last element of the work job description is the data retrieval box. This box is always located in the lower right hand corner so that retrieval of the data on each client can be obtained easily by simply lifting the corner of each successive description (See Figure 3, Section D). This box contains three essential elements always written in the same order. The code identifies the job number which is assigned to each job description for computer data analysis or brevity if the job descriptions are to be plotted by hand. The second element is the amount of tokens earned which is utilized primarily to determine the number of tokens a client has in his possession at any time. The final element of this section is the percentage of correctly completed steps or objectives. The percentage section over time will allow for a percentage plot of each completed or partially completed description which can be used diagnostically at a later date to determine work areas which are sufficient or insufficient for movement to the next level or eventual job placement.

CENTER FOR DEVELOPMENTAL AND LEARNING DISORDERS
TOKEN ECONOMY

10-22-71   **DUPLICATING MACHINE OPERATOR**
TOKEN VALUE 3 PER ½ HOUR

NAME_____

DATE_____

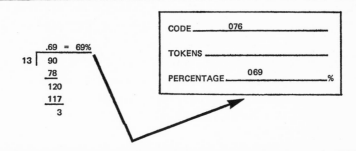

$$\frac{.69\ =\ 69\%}{13\ |\ 90}$$

13 | 90
     78
    120
    117
      3

CODE _____ 076 _____

TOKENS _____

PERCENTAGE ____ 069 ____%

Figure 4. The percentage calculation for the work job description in Figure 3.

The job description should be arranged in a characteristic manner as previously outlined and should be standard in the sense that the key items are not in different places for different descriptions. This standardization ensures against error in the identification of pertinent information on the part of the supervisor and client. The standardization allows for easy verification as to correctness or accuracy on the part of the supervisor if verification personnel are available. The uniformity of job descriptions also reduces the amount of errors that can be made in the retrieval of data from these job descriptions.

The client who cannot read will be assisted by the use of key words on the description and the description objectives. The description read to a

CENTER FOR DEVELOPMENTAL AND LEARNING DISORDERS

TOKEN ECONOMY

1-21-72

NAME_____

DATE_____

CURRENT EVENTS

TOKEN VALUE   2

YES | NO

⊥_____   TWO (2) TOKENS FOR THREE (3) NEWSPAPER CLIPPINGS.

CODE_____196_____

TOKENS_____

PERCENTAGE_____%

Figure 5. Current events section of an academic job description.

client a number of times will allow the nonreading client the opportunity to identify key words until he can work the description without supervision.

THE ACADEMIC JOB DESCRIPTIONS

The basic academic job descriptions consist of the date on which the job description was last revised, the client's name and date in the top right hand corner, and three essential academic parts. The first is current events with the description title and token value centered in the middle. The current events section is a " 'yes', 'no' " item determining whether or not the client brought three newspaper clippings from the newspaper of the previous night (See Figure 5). The current events section can be done the first thing every morning so as to build student-teacher rapport as well as to keep the client abreast of local and world happenings. A current events section is essentially a one-step job description, and the percentage is figured 0 percent or 100 percent. If the code is never-changing, as is the case here, it can be made part of the existing job descriptions thereby lessening the amount of writing to be done by supervisor or client. Attention should be given to the fact that even though this description contains three descriptions in one, it is essentially the same format as the work job description. The next section in academics is reading; this description is broken down into thirty-minute segments to capitalize upon the effects of immediate reinforcement. The token value ranges from one to five within a thirty-minute period as indicated by the token value section (Figure 6, Section A).

Many clients may spend as many as seven 30-minute periods in academics,

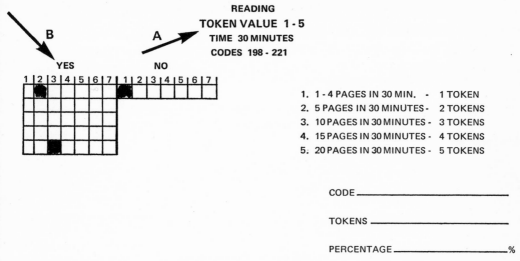

READING
TOKEN VALUE 1 - 5
TIME 30 MINUTES
CODES 198 - 221

1. 1 - 4 PAGES IN 30 MIN.   -   1 TOKEN
2. 5 PAGES IN 30 MINUTES -   2 TOKENS
3. 10 PAGES IN 30 MINUTES -   3 TOKENS
4. 15 PAGES IN 30 MINUTES -   4 TOKENS
5. 20 PAGES IN 30 MINUTES -   5 TOKENS

CODE _____

TOKENS _____

PERCENTAGE _____%

Figure 6. Reading section of an academic job description.

so the description may be sectioned off into the number of thirty-minute periods per day as shown in Figure 6, Section B. For the first period a person may earn zero to five tokens. No attempt at the material and no reading done would ensure that the client would be paid no tokens and number one under the "No" section would be filled in (See Figure 6, Section B).

The client who reads from one to four pages would receive one token, and the first square under period number two would be filled in. The client who reads twenty pages in period number three would receive five tokens and the square would be filled in as marked in Figure 6, Section B.

Each subsequent thirty-minute period could be darkened according to the client's performance. The maximum number of tokens that could be earned would be five for a thirty-minute period or thirty-five for seven 30-minute periods of academic work. If all of the seven squares were filled in, it would reveal a graphic description of the client's performance during each thirty-minute period.

This graphic information could then be utilized diagnostically to determine the most productive times of day to assign this client to academics. The client who consistently gets "no" checks in periods number one and number two and demonstrates a continual increase in academic performance for the remainder of the day could easily be channeled into a work activity during the first two periods and assigned to academics for periods number three through seven (See Figure 7).

The code, number of tokens earned, and percentage figures are to be calculated as a total for the day. The client who earns one token for each of the periods one through five would be paid five tokens and receive a per-

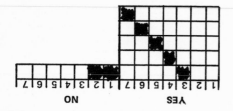

NOTE THAT IF THE CHART IS TURNED UPSIDE DOWN YOU HAVE A GRAPH SLANTING TO THE LEFT WHICH MEANS AN INCREASE IN PRODUCTIVITY IN ACADEMICS AS THE DAY PROGRESSES.

Figure 7. Graphic information on most productive periods of the day.

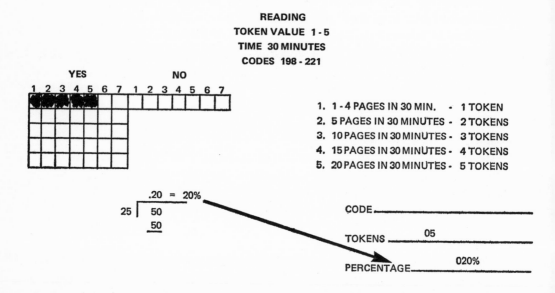

READING
TOKEN VALUE 1 - 5
TIME 30 MINUTES
CODES 198 - 221

1. 1 - 4 PAGES IN 30 MIN. - 1 TOKEN
2. 5 PAGES IN 30 MINUTES - 2 TOKENS
3. 10 PAGES IN 30 MINUTES - 3 TOKENS
4. 15 PAGES IN 30 MINUTES - 4 TOKENS
5. 20 PAGES IN 30 MINUTES - 5 TOKENS

CODE _____

TOKENS ____05_____

PERCENTAGE ___020%_____

IF A CLIENT READ 20 PAGES PER 30 MINUTE PERIOD FOR 5 PERIODS, HE COULD EARN A MAXIMUM OF 25 TOKENS. TOTAL POSSIBLE DIVIDED INTO AMOUNT EARNED GIVES THE PERCENTAGE.

Figure 8. Percentage figured on Reading Job Description for five 30-minute periods.

centage of twenty (See Figure 8). This percentage is easily calculated by dividing the number of tokens possible into the actual obtained number.

The codes for this section may range from 198 to 221. Code 198, 199 and 200 would be indicative of prereading materials whereas codes 201 through 221 would be the identification of particular books or levels of materials (See Chapter 8). The utilization of the Sullivan Programmed Reading Series published by McGraw-Hill Book Company is recommended for use.

Superficially, the job description may indicate a strong concentration or amount of material read rather than accuracy in what is read. The materials used should be of the programmed instruction type which utilizes immediate feedback as a learning mechanism and offers periodic tests of accuracy. Behavioral objectives for each book or each level of reading material should also be established so as to maximize effective utilization of the material and ensure that learning has actually taken place.

The math section of this job description is exactly the same as the reading section except the word *problems* is substituted for the word *pages* and, of course, the codes differ. The utilization of the word *problems* not only distinguishes the two sections for the client, but requires that an entire page of math problems be completed. The material recommended for utilization is the Sullivan Programmed Math Series published by Behavioral Research Laboratories, Palo Alto, California. The codes would be assigned according to the book the client was in or the level of performance of the client.

As on the previous work job description, the academic job description is figured as three separate job descriptions; tokens and percentage are figured as separate earnings (See Appendix D for a complete academic job description).

With the utilization of programmed instruction materials, the inevitable question of cheating or unsuccessful completion of the number of pages read arises. A criterion of some type must be assigned to the amount of pages read so as to ensure successful mastery of the material. One answer to this problem may be the utilization of periodic tests of material mastery with a test at the end of each book to ascertain proficiency at handling the material and concepts taught. Another solution would be to allow the client to read aloud so that the supervisor is sure to positively reinforce appropriate reading.

The Sullivan Programmed Reading Series is easily adaptable to a behavioral checklist which can be given or checked upon the completion of a book level. Upon purchasing this material, a complete listing of each minute item to be taught by book level can be obtained through the publisher. This information can then easily be converted into a behavioral checklist as behavioral objectives, and a criterion can be set for determining a mastery level. If 80 percent of the objectives are not met, the client can be required to repeat the book or complete supplementary material. Figure 9 shows objectives for books number one, two, three and four.

SUCCESS CRITERION OBJECTIVES
BOOK I

Yes **No**

_____ _____ 1. When presented with a visual stimulus, can name the following letters: n,f,c,s,b,g,d,C,T,S,M,P,D.

_____ _____ 2. When presented with a visual stimulus, can sound the following letters or letter combinations: n,f,c,s,b,g,d,C,T,N,S,M,P,D,th,ng,sh.

_____ _____ 3. Can correctly name from visual presentation the following words: Thin, fat, fan, can, cat, sit, this, is, tab, Nip, Sam, on, sing, pant, sat, Ann, hat, his, that, fit, ham, the, hit, him, mint, ship, fish, fast, Miss Pat, dish, and, sad, did, hand, had, pig, on.

_____ _____ 4. When presented orally, can spell the following words: (same as in No. 3 above).

_____ _____ 5. Can demonstrate knowledge of the possessive 's by rewriting five sentences into possessives: e.g. The hat belongs to Paul. Paul's hat

_____ _____ 6. When presented with an oral stimulus of a proper name, can write down that name beginning with a capital letter.

_____ _____ 7. Can demonstrate knowledge of the suffix ing (present participle) by rewriting five simple sentences from the simple present tense to the present participle: e.g. He runs. He is running.

_____ _____ 8. Can demonstrate knowledge of the suffix s as it is used in the present tense singular form by rewriting the infinitive form into the present tense, singular.

to run	He runs.
to cook	He cooks.
to sit	He sits.

_____ _____ 9. Can demonstrate knowledge of the suffix s as it is used in plural nouns by writing the following nouns in plural form:

e.g.	cat	cats
	mint	mints
	ship	ships
	hat	hats
	pig	pigs

SUCCESS CRITERION OBJECTIVES
BOOK II

Yes **No**

_____ _____ 1. When presented with a visual stimulus, student can name the following letters: r, k, l, h, b, e.

_____ _____ 2. When presented with a visual stimulus, student can sound the following letters or letter combinations: r, k, e, l, h, b, ch, tch, ck.

_____ _____ 3. When presented with a visual stimulus, student can correctly name the following words: dig, sand, sniff, bag, sandman, big, bat, bit, stand, bang, band, tap, snap, sting, fin, rat, ran, rag, rip, trip, past, sand, ring, ding, rang, drip, print, chin, rich, catch, trap, patch, match, scratch, kit, kitten, mitten, bring, to, kitchen, tack, sack, back, chicken, lap, lip, lick, pink, red, bed, dress, best.

_____ _____ 4. When presented with an oral stimulus, student can correctly spell the following words: (same as in No. 3 above)

_____ _____ 5. Can demonstrate proper use of the comma and exclamation mark by choosing correct punctuation mark in 10 sentences.

Figure 9. Behavioral checklist for programmed reading series.

_____ _____ 6. Can demonstrate knowledge of suffix -en by correctly spelling chicken, kitchen, kitten, mitten.

SUCCESS CRITERION OBJECTIVES
BOOK III

Yes   No
_____ _____ 1. When presented with a visual stimulus, can name the consonant w.
_____ _____ 2. When presented with a visual stimulus, can sound the consonant w.
_____ _____ 3. Can demonstrate knowledge of contractions I'll, I'm, that's by correctly rewriting the following two word combinations into contractions:

I will	I'll
I am	I'm
that is	that's

_____ _____ 4. When presented with a visual stimulus, can name the following words:

pill	pick	track	get
up	pack	black	tell
Meg	Bill	bank	sell
fill	Dick	blank	men
glad	grass	milkman	them
glass	sick	drank	will
milk	kick	still	I'll
sink	stick	well	I'm
drink	brick	wig	that's
spill	crack	with	went
spell	skip	crash	splash
bill	into	wet	up

_____ _____ 5. When presented with an auditory stimulus, can correctly spell the following words: (See No. 4 above.)

SUCCESS CRITERION OBJECTIVES
BOOK IV

Yes   No
_____ _____ 1. Can correctly name from visual presentation the letter v.
_____ _____ 2. Can correctly sound from visual presentation the letter v.
_____ _____ 3. Can correctly write from auditory presentation the letter v.
_____ _____ 4. Can correctly pronounce and spell from visual presentation the 37 new words presented in Book 4.
_____ _____ 5. Can demonstrate the usage of double g by correctly spelling egg.
_____ _____ 6. Can demonstrate the use of ed suffix of the past tense of verbs by writing correctly the past tense of the 3 verbs: rip, beg, hand.
_____ _____ 7. Can demonstrate the use of final silent e which does not affect the value of syllable vowel by correctly reading give and live.

Figure 9. Behavioral checklist for programmed reading series—continued

SELF-HELP JOB DESCRIPTION

The self-help job descriptions are job descriptions which are not particularly related to the completion of a job, but are related to economically useful domestically related activities. These are behaviors which are vital in becoming a self-reliant citizen. A girl, in order to be a successful homemaker, must know how to sew, make beds, cook, clean, and care for her physical appearance. The indigent client who is mentally retarded and without parents must know how to wash clothes and maintain his living quarters to such a degree as to be economically useful to himself. All clients need not be assigned these descriptions except in an initial screening procedure to determine the degree of need for these types of behaviors.

A client found to have a deficient repertoire of self-help behaviors may be assigned to activities in a daily living unit or vocational home economics area which could follow the same job description format as the work job description. The client could then learn more easily the basic behaviors of maintaining and caring for his own personal needs (See Appendices for examples of self-help descriptions).

AUXILIARY WORK JOB DESCRIPTION

In the same light as the self-help job description, the auxiliary work job description is intended for the shaping of behaviors which are auxiliary to work but are not teaching specific work behaviors. The utilization of the time clock which has become a standard in industry for hourly wages is a perfect example of behaviors which are auxiliary to work. Other auxiliary behaviors such as grooming and punctuality are also essential to holding a good job.

Punctuality

The punctuality job description is a marked deviation from other types of descriptions in that punctuality should be reinforced when and where it occurs. A client may have to report to numerous areas during the day and each incidence of punctual behavior should be positively reinforced. Certain portions of the day will have standard times of arrival such as the day's beginning, reporting from lunch, and reporting from break as shown in Figure 10, Section A. Each job description could then vary, depending on the number of areas to which a client must report (See Figure 10, Section B).

The punctuality description can be carried by the client from area to area so that duplication of punctuality data by area does not occur. Printing the description on cardstock rather than standard paper prevents destruction of the description through manipulation and makes the card easy to fit into a shirt pocket or purse. This procedure ensures that the client will take the card from area to area in order to obtain a token for being on time. However, if the client receives no remuneration for turning in the card, that day's data will be lost or difficult to obtain after he has reported to the last area for the day's activities.

The solution to this problem would be to add supplementary data to this

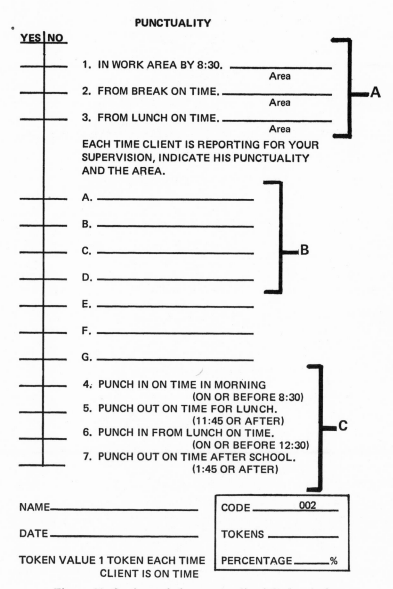

Figure 10. Sections of the punctuality job description.

card in the afternoon which are steps four, five, six and seven in Figure 10, Section C. Procedures such as these would ensure that the card would be' taken to each area, as well as deposited in a central location in the afternoon. A convenient procedure could be worked out to include "punctuality" and "use of the time clock" on one side of the card. The other side could include

CENTER FOR DEVELOPMENTAL AND LEARNING DISORDERS

TOKEN ECONOMY

PUNCTUALITY

YES	NO		
	✓	1. IN WORK AREA BY 8:30.	Sr. High Class
			Area
✓		2. FROM BREAK ON TIME.	June 29, 1973
			Area
✓		3. FROM LUNCH ON TIME.	June 29, 1973
			Area

EACH TIME CLIENT IS REPORTING FOR YOUR SUPERVISION, INDICATE HIS PUNCTUALITY AND THE AREA.

YES	NO		
✓		A.	Resource Room
✓		B.	Activities of Daily Living
		C.	
		D.	
		E.	
		F.	
		G.	
	✓	4. PUNCH IN ON TIME IN MORNING (ON OR BEFORE 8:30)	
✓		5. PUNCH OUT ON TIME FOR LUNCH. (11:45 OR AFTER)	
✓		6. PUNCH IN FROM LUNCH ON TIME. (ON OR BEFORE 12:30)	
✓		7. PUNCH OUT ON TIME AFTER SCHOOL. (1:45 OR AFTER)	

NAME John Doe

DATE

TOKEN VALUE 1 TOKEN EACH TIME CLIENT IS ON TIME

CODE 002

TOKENS 07

PERCENTAGE 078 %

Figure 11. Completed punctuality job description.

the use of the time clock behaviors irrespective of time. The use of the time clock by time and for correctly punching could be paid for in the afternoon upon the completion of all time punches for the day. The above-mentioned procedure would ensure the collection of both the use of the time clock and punctuality data at the day's end. Figure 11 is a completed punctuality card.

The Grooming Job Description

The grooming job description is also a behavior which is auxiliary to work yet a definite requirement for securing and maintaining adequate employment. The grooming description is one of the most difficult job descriptions to write without placing value judgments on what does or does not constitute good grooming. Subjectively, the description could be written including only personal judgments of what constitutes good grooming. However, a more empirical approach to the problem would be a quick survey of employers within the community to ascertain requirements for employees in the grooming category. This procedure would eliminate the subjective value judgments on the part of the supervisor as well as offer a valid criteria for each objective.

Grooming is a measure which will vary according to the type of job and time of day the measure is taken. Therefore, the best procedure for checking the grooming job description is to require that it be taken upon arrival to begin work and not be retaken until the next day. A procedure of this type would ensure that and emphasize the need for a client to report to work well-groomed. All job descriptions of the auxiliary category are extremely objective, with the exception of grooming where a certain degree of personal opinion is required. The grooming job description does limit the supervisor to only those areas which are outlined on the description which reduces subjectivity to a minimum.

Before the supervisor may dismiss his client as having completed a job, he must calculate the percentage as previously demonstrated by dividing the number of correctly completed steps by the total number of steps on the job description. An additional calculation is also required to figure total tokens earned. This is accomplished by taking a percentage of the token value of the job description. This calculation can take a great deal of staff time and is subject to error in calculation. A handy reference chart which provides ease in calculating percentages earned and total tokens earned is essential in reducing supervisor time and effort as well as eliminating human error in the calculation process. As shown in Figure 12, a person who receives five "yes" checks out of the possible eight steps of the grooming job description would receive two tokens and a percentage value of sixty-two. The calculation of this information is a simple process when a chart is devised with these calculations already figured.

CENTER FOR DEVELOPMENTAL AND LEARNING DISORDERS

TOKEN ECONOMY

2-9-72   NAME _____

DATE _____

GROOMING

TOKEN VALUE 4

YES	NO	
✓		1. CLEAN HAIR A. NO OBVIOUS DANDRUFF B. NON-GREASY (GIRLS) C. NO EXCESSIVE HAIR TONIC (BOYS)
✓		2. HAIR NEATLY COMBED
	✓	3. BODY CLEANLINESS A. CLEAN TEETH B. CLEAN ARMS (NO OBVIOUS MATERIAL) C. CLEAN HANDS AND REASONABLE NEAT AND CLEAN FINGERNAILS D. CLEAN EARS
	✓	4. NO BODY ODOR
✓		5. CLEAN AND NEATLY PRESSED CLOTHES (NO OBVIOUS DIRT OR EXCESSIVE WRINKLES)
✓		6. CLEAN SHOES (FREE OF DIRT OR DUST — NOT OBVIOUSLY DIRTY)
	✓	7. CLEAN SHAVEN (BOYS) SHAVEN LEGS AND UNDERARMS (ALL VISIBLE HAIR ON LEGS SHOULD BE REMOVED — GIRLS)
✓		8. NATURAL LOOKING AND NEATLY APPLIED MAKE-UP (GIRLS) SOCKS (BOYS)

CODE _____ 003 _____	
TOKENS _____ 02 _____	
PERCENTAGE _____ 062 _____ %	

Figure 12. Completed grooming job description.

Figure 13 can be utilized to reduce supervisors' time and effort in calcula-tion. The percentage may be figured by referring to the *number of checks on the job description* section of Figure 13. Proceed from left to right to the column marked number eight which is the number of checks on the

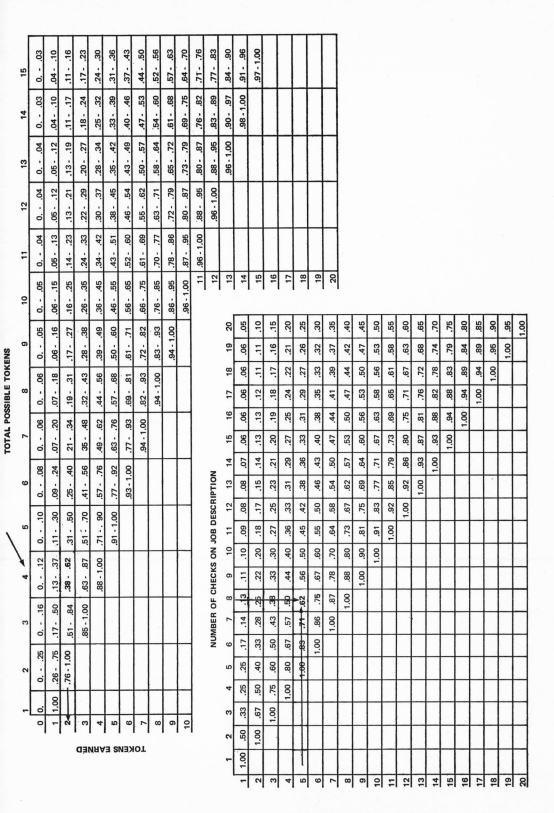

Figure 13. Percentage chart.

grooming job description. Proceed five squares down column eight which corresponds to the *number of yes checks obtained*. This square reflects a percentage of sixty-two.

In order to determine the number of tokens earned, go to the *total possible tokens* section of the chart (note that the grooming job description has a token value of four). Proceed from left to right to the fourth column and drop down three squares until the 62 percent figure is reached. Read back across the chart to *total tokens earned* which in this case is two.

This procedure is easily learned and extremely effective in reducing the time interval between the client's completion of the job and subsequent issuance of the token.

The client may have difficulty understanding the calculation process, and it may be explained in a positive manner to reduce the punishment aspect of the economy. Praise for the number of "yes" checks and ignoring, or at least not calling attention to, the "no" check is important, especially if generalized attention is positively reinforcing to the client.

CHAPTER 5

THE EXCHANGE SYSTEM

THE PRIMARY PURPOSE of the utilization of a secondary reinforcing system is to allow the client to choose his own positive reinforcers. The secondary system allows the client access to almost any primary reward by exchanging the secondary reinforcer (token) for the primary rewards which he desires. By offering a large milieu of possible reinforcers, the program is sure to identify appropriate rewards on a personalized basis.

The system can be manipulated so as to ascertain the rewards which are most popular. The most popular rewards then can be the most expensive in exchange. The concept of supply and demand operates in this system as it does in the exchange that is used in American society. The token economy is nothing more than society in miniature with special modifications of requirements to such a degree as to ensure that learning takes place. The difference between society and a token economy is only that requirements for earning power are made contingent upon behaviors that have not been learned, whereas in society money is paid for skills already learned. The discussion of construction of job descriptions in Chapters 3 and 4 points markedly to the difference in the American economy and a simulation of the American economy which is being proposed here.

The utilization of a secondary reinforcing system or a learned reinforcer are many. The primary one is the assurance of the client's finding the consequence of his behavior which he will work to obtain.

THE TOKEN

The question may arise as to the reason for not using regular currency or a simulation of regular currency for the token. The token economy system being the same exchange system or a simulation of the exchange utilized in the United States should in theory parallel what is in the real world. However, certain problems exist with the utilization of United States currency which makes it unusable in a token economy system.

United States currency can be stolen, as evidenced by the large number of thefts in the past few years. The United States currency is only identifiable by a serial number which, when used in another part of the country, is extremely difficult to trace. Another important factor is that a simulation of United States currency could be counterfeited which would definitely upset the economic balance. The introduction of coins presents an even more difficult problem in that if stolen, they are impossible to trace. Two types of monetary exchange within the United States are not hampered with the above-mentioned problems. These are the cashier's check or money order and the traveler's check. A device which simulates one of these two exchange systems would be the most productive in the utilization of a token economy.

A paper token, like a cashier's check, made out to the client with his name, the date, and the supervisor's name who issued the token would alleviate many problems associated with the utilization of currency which simulates the United States exchange note. The paper token would eliminate anyone else spending the token because it could only be spent by the person to whom it was issued (Logan, 1970) (See Figure 14, Section A). The client could not hoard the token if a stipulation were written on the token as to how long it carried the value listed. (See Figure 14, Section B). Most of all, the paper token could not be stolen, traded or borrowed because a supervisor had to attach his signature as proof that the token was earned by the named client. (See Figure 14, Section C). The procedure would ensure that a token spent by a client was a token earned through adequate work performance by that client. Numerous commercial tokens are available; however, the buyer has to be extremely cautious that the tokens purchased from commercial companies do not carry the inherent problems previously mentioned.

The token itself can become a data collection device which could be diagnostically useful to the client. If the paper token is printed on different colored paper for the different types of areas the client is asigned to, or if

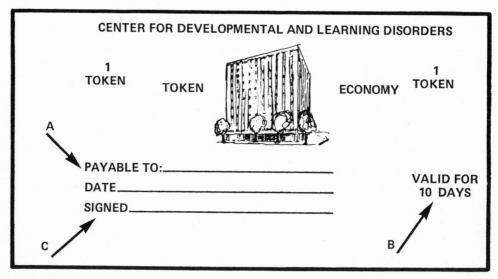

Figure 14. Sections of the paper token.

the picture on the token is so distributed that a different picture is on every denomination, this too can be helpful. A quick glance by the supervisor of the amount of tokens earned by color would be indicative of where the subject's earning power was. An example may be if a client reports to academics, a work area, and a self-help area, a supervisor may quickly glance at the client's accumulated total to determine the amount by color. The supervisor would then be able to verbally praise the client for his splendid performance in academics because he had so many green colored tokens.

A program analysis of collected tokens over time would give a rough estimate of the client's performance in any area to which he has been assigned. If all of one client's tokens in academics are of the five denomination, a supervisor may ascertain that the client is earning a maximum rate every thirty minutes in academics and has an excellent performance in that area (See academic job description, Chapter 4).

The use of the paper token can also create evaluation types of jobs. The construction, printing, cutting, distribution and collection of the paper token can all be divided into job descriptions for that work behavior. If the primary objective of a program is not just training *per se,* but evaluation of job performance as well, a person may be evaluated on this job as well as he could be evaluated on any other.

The construction of many of the charts, graphs, scoring sheets, and other paraphernalia needed for the operation of the token economy provides excellent evaluation instruments for which job descriptions may be written and evaluations of work performance made.

The *Not Valid After 10 Days* section of the paper token requires that the paper token be deposited in a banking account which saves the client from loosing, by expiration, the tokens earned and thereby positively reinforces banking behavior. Banking behavior is, of course, a self-help skill which would be required for adequately handling one's money in the real world.

THE CHECK

In order for a banking system to be most effective, money should be deposited and withdrawn with the utilization of a checking system. The checks, too, must be individualized so as not to allow clients to borrow or utilize checks that were purchased as a reward by another client. The easiest way to alleviate this situation is to issue personalized checks. Personalized checks would then require that the holder have the same name as the printed indication on the checkbook. To be an adequate simulation of a real life situation, the checks should cost and the client should pay for the banking service, unless the money is deposited into a savings account, and, of course, to many individuals saving is a reinforcing contingency. The client case number could be printed on the personalized checks as his account number, and this

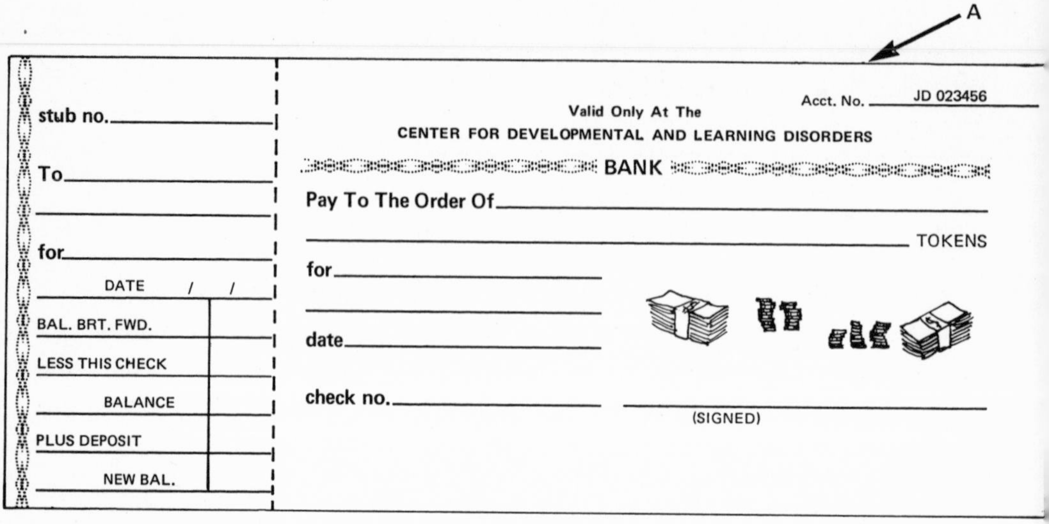
A

stub no.

To

for

DATE / /

BAL. BRT. FWD.

LESS THIS CHECK

BALANCE

PLUS DEPOSIT

NEW BAL.

Acct. No. JD 023456

Valid Only At The

CENTER FOR DEVELOPMENTAL AND LEARNING DISORDERS

BANK

Pay To The Order Of

TOKENS

for

date

check no.

(SIGNED)

Figure 15. Token economy check.

number would only correspond to the subject's account number; funds would not be withdrawn from any other account (See Figure 15, Section A).

THE BANK

The bank is an essential element in establishing and maintaining an adequate token economy system. An easy deposit and withdrawal system which is accurate and reliable will ensure that the clients can rely on the banking procedure, whereas a faulty accounting procedure may be sufficiently punitive to eliminate banking behavior from a client's repertoire. The bank must be available; that is, banking hours must be established and adhered to with dogmatic accuracy. The bank must also be established as a reinforcing agent; that is, tokens should be paid to the client from the bank. This procedure will, through association, establish that the bank is a nice place to visit or that the bank is where good things happen. The punishment aspect of not having enough tokens to purchase a particular item should be minimized and alternative items should be issued by the bank tellers so as to ensure that reinforcement occurs during banking time rather than punishment.

Several devices can be extremely helpful in eliminating problems which can occur at banking. A tally sheet as shown in Figure 16 with the client's name, case number or code, and a listing of various reinforcing contingencies along with a section for deposits and withdrawals is extremely helpful in making accurate banking transactions. If the transactions are then placed into codes, very little space is required to record daily transactions. All transactions can be recorded on one or two of these sheets per day. The reinforcing contingencies, withdrawals and deposits can then be sectioned into two parts marked *T* and *C*. By merely recording the transaction under *T* (token) or *C* (check) a determination can be made of the type of transaction made. The bank can also make a recording of the types of transactions which have occurred by code so that a quick determination can be made of what items were purchased by all clients during the day. Codes for specific reinforcing contingencies can be written on the reverse side of the banking sheet.

WHAT CAN BE PURCHASED

Nearly any item that the subject desires that is within reason should be made part of allowable purchases. The types of things which can be made available at minimal costs to the program are listed in Figure 17. The listing here, of course, is a limited one; and the client should be allowed to purchase almost any item that he will work to obtain unless it is illegal, immoral, or grossly improper. The client's desire for a particular item could also set the value for that item. An extremely desired item would cost more than a not so relished item.

SICK LEAVE

One of the listed items on the reinforcing contingency list is absences. Absenteeism is an extremely important factor in maintaining adequate employment. Also, if the worker is absent, he reduces his earning potential greatly. A difficulty that may be encountered is what should be done about an absence. To approach this question from a positive standpoint is extremely important due primarily to the fact that if a subject is punished for being absent, it only adds to the fact that school or training programs are not only punishing because the work is difficult and academics are intolerable, but the people even punish you when you are sick.

The reinforcing contingency sheet lists a charge of twenty tokens for absence. It is extremely difficult for a person who is without a surplus of tokens to re-enter a program after an extended illness and have to pay twenty tokens for each day of absence whether due to illness or some other reason. Therefore, a policy needs to be established so as to reinforce presence rather than punish absence. A quick scan of the real working world will give you a solution to this dilemma. This is the concept of sick leave.

A person may accumulate so many days of sick leave by earning them due to presence on the job. For example: If a person works twenty straight days without being absent, he then can earn one day sick leave which would give him, in essence, a free day which would cover almost any minor illness.

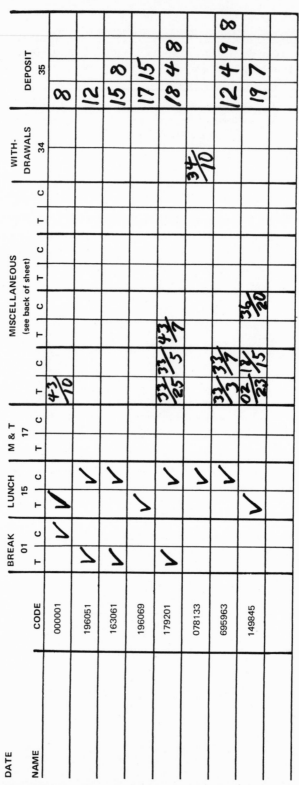

Figure 16. Banking ledger of daily token economy transactions.

BANKING CODES
Effective September 29, 1973

01 — Morning Break .... 10 tokens
02 — Token Exchange .... Various
03 — Coke, Coffee—Beverage .... Various
04 — Radio—Group Time (While Working) .... 5 per 30 minutes
05 — Redeem Punctuality Card if Lost .... 2 tokens
06 — Purchase New Punctuality Card .... 5 tokens
07 — Individual Radio Time (With Quiet Time) .... 10 per 30 minutes
08 — Individual Radio Time (While Working) .... 5 per 30 minutes
09 — Pencils .... 5 tokens per pencil
10 — Ball Point Pen .... 25 tokens per pen
11 — Paper .... 20 tokens per tablet
12 — Purchase New Time Card .... 5 tokens
13 —
14 —
15 — Lunch .... 20 tokens
16 — Out to Lunch .... 60 tokens
17 — Maintenance and Transportation Check .... 35 tokens
18 — Checkbook .... 15 tokens
19 — Redeem Time Card if Not in "Out" Rack .... 5 tokens
20 — Day Absent (Without Insurance or Sick Leave) .... 20 tokens
21 — Day Off .... 80 tokens
22 — Counseling .... 8 tokens per 15 minutes
23 — Use of the Telephone .... 5 per call—10 min. limit
24 — Recreation .... 5 per 15 minutes
25 — Payment for Preferred Job .... Various
26 —
27 —
28 —
29 —
30 — Quiet Time .... 10 per 30 minutes
31 —
32 —
33 — Television Time .... 10 per 30 minutes
34 — Withdrawals ....
35 — Deposits ....
36 — Driver Education (Behind the Wheel) .... 20 per 30 minutes
37 —
38 —
39 — Leaving Early (sick, emergency, catch bus, etc.) ...... Various
40 — Wash, Roll, Dry, and Comb Hair .... 5 tokens
41 — Cut Hair .... 5 tokens
42 — Purchase New Bus Card .... 50 tokens
43 — Canteen ....
44 — Insurance (10 Tokens Issuance Fee) .... 20 per month

Figure 17. Partial listing of reinforcing contingencies.

These days could be accumulated over a year's period of time. However, the problem is still apparent if a worker has an extended illness.

Workman's Compensation Insurance

The problem of extended illness or hospitalization again can be answered by real world situations. The person who is employed on a job that pays a limited amount of money may resort to fringe benefits which would be helpful in the event of an unexpected accident or illness. The rehabilitation program can establish an insurance arrangement whereby the client is paid for absences due to illness for each day of his absence beyond his sick leave by merely selling an insurance policy and requiring that the client maintain the premiums.

TOKEN ECONOMY

INSURANCE POLICY

Policyholder John Doe	Date of Issuance April 20th, 19_____
Authorized by: J. Driskill	Issuance Fee 10 tokens

The holder of this policy is entitled to the benefits named herein and agrees to pay the monthly premium as stated in Section III.

I.   When policyholder is absent from the CDLD program over and above the accumulated number of sick leave days, this policy will pay the TOKEN ECONOMY BANK the indebtedness incurred by the policyholder.

II.   This policy will only pay for days sick with proper doctor's excuse.

III.   Rate of this policy: 20 tokens per month payable on or before the 10th day of each month (or the Monday following if the 10th day falls on Saturday or Sunday).

John Doe
Signature of Insured

Figure 18. Token economy insurance policy.

CHAPTER 6

HOW THE PROGRAM WORKS

A CLIENT IS REFERRED for evaluation in your program. The referral information indicates that he has a 65 IQ, is a product of a broken home, and lives in a federal housing project. Medical information on this client reflects no significant anomalies with the retardation etiology unknown. The client's academic background reflects one of constant failure with a history of being expelled from three different schools. Attempts to gain employment have all met with failure primarily due to the fact that he never obained an education beyond the sixth grade. However, his academic skills reflect even lower achievement levels than is reflected by the sixth grade academic classification.

This client's case material should be reviewed by a referral committee or screening committee and, if deemed an appropriate case for your particular program, should be brought before staffing to ascertain as many opinions as possible in order to determine the benefit the program can have toward the rehabilitation of this client. Staff would then agree as to the status of this client and, if accepted, would refer him to diagnostic areas for evaluation. The client should be first evaluated in academics since this seems to be his primary difficulty. He then should be evaluated in vocational areas. This procedure would entail administering educational achievement batteries, individual intelligence tests, and vocational competency batteries. During this evaluation period, baseline information would be taken on the client for token economy purposes; that is, he would receive no tokens during this period of time, but would have data taken on him as if he were on the token economy. The baseline period would then give an indication of subsequent improvement when the incentive system is instituted some three weeks later. The evaluation procedure should be completed at the end of at least one month, and the client's case then would return to staffing. The results of the diagnostic workup should be discussed and a determination made as to the areas required to improve his deficit skills and enhance the observed strengths reported from the evaluation period.

Assume the information was reported to staff and an agreement was reached that the client should continue in academics in order to improve his basic academic skills of reading and math. Also assume that the client is in need of transportation and should be evaluated and included in the driver education training program. The behaviors dissonant with continuous employment were observed to be inability to stick with a task until completed, continual talking with other clients while working, and attempts to complete the job which were poorly done or omitted. The primary problem noted, however, was the fact that the client was extremely slow with all the details of the job, but extremely fast with finishing or completing the task.

Staff should then recommend that the client be placed on the token economy system in academics and driver education and special attention should be paid to work behaviors of the auxiliary type. A case coordinator would be assigned to the client and this staff member should explain in detail the requirements and the payoff for achieving these requirements in each area to which the client is assigned.

A typical day would reflect the client reporting to the time clock before 8:30 A.M. and punching in before that time. He would then report to academics or the academic work area before 8:30 A.M. and pick up a punctuality card which, when submitted to his supervisor of that area, would earn him one token. He will carry this card with him during the entire day; whenever he reports to an area on time, the card is checked, and he receives one token. If he reports late, the client's card is checked and no token is issued. He receives no verbal abasement or no comment whatsoever as to the reason for being late; he just does not receive a token.

He then obtains a grooming sheet and checks this job description by himself. The supervisor then checks his and all other clients' grooming according to the steps outlined on the description. If the client has a mustache, for example, but all other grooming checks are "yes," the description would then reflect that he completed all the tasks except one and received a percentage of eighty-seven; and he has lost one token because he is not clean-shaven.

When the client delivers to the supervisor three newspaper clippings from the paper of the night before, he receives a percentage of 100 and 2 tokens. Along with the token issuance comes a barrage of verbal praise and physical contact for having done what was required and earning tokens at a satisfactory rate. The supervisor then discusses with the class the most interesting of the articles presented to him by this client's classmates. This procedure continues until 9:00 A.M. at which time a timer is set and work begins on the reading level to which each client is presently working. If clients do not deliver newspaper articles, they would have to go from 8:30 A.M. until 9:00 A.M. without earning any tokens except for grooming and punctuality. The academic program is completely individualized with members of the class ranging from prereader to seventh grade reading levels.

The client in question begins reading at nine o'clock for the thirty-minute period on the book level to which he is assigned; while reading, he is constantly receiving positive social reinforcement for appropriate behaviors. If he is idle or lackadaisical in his approach to reading, he is ignored until appropriate behavior is observed, and the supervisor then gives him a pat on the back and a verbal statement of praise. The supervisor verbally states how proud he is of the client's work behavior.

A timer bell rings at the end of the thirty-minute period, and each of the clients from the classroom receives the number of tokens which his behavior earned for him in that time period. The client in question reads five pages the first thirty-minute period from 9:00 A.M. until 9:30 A.M. and receives two tokens. The timer bell is then reset to expire at 10:00 A.M. This thirty-minute period allows the client an opportunity to improve his performance over the last thirty-minute period, and he is greatly encouraged to do just that.

The timer bell rings at 10:00 A.M. and the hypothetical client has exceeded his past effort and earns four tokens for having completed fifteen pages. The 10:00 A.M. timer also is a prompt for the 10:00 A.M. break period which can be obtained by paying ten tokens; however, the client in question does not elect to attend break and will save his tokens to ensure that lunch can be purchased.

The 10:00 A.M. until 10:30 A.M. period allows time for more academics and, of course, he is switched from reading material to math material. The math material is again totally individualized and in sequential programmed instruction books. Our hypothetical client does four pages of arithmetic for which he earns one token. The timer bell rings at 10:30 A.M., which not only brings the one token but also an opportunity to improve the performance exhibited over the last thirty-minute period.

When the 11:00 A.M. bell rings, our client has received two additional tokens for having improved his performance over the last period by five pages. The supervisor then requires that he report to the resource room or teaching machine room in order to receive supplementary instruction in the utilization of phonics. His punctuality card is signed in section *A* to reflect that he is to report to the resource room by 11:05 A.M. Upon reporting, the resource room supervisor checks his punctuality card at 11:03 A.M.; he receives one token for being punctual.

He is assigned then to the task of completing the assigned phonics material to an acceptable criterion level. He then completes the assigned material and earns 50 percent and two tokens for first period. He then works for another twenty-five-minute period and earns 80 percent of the total possible tokens or three tokens. He receives five tokens for the fifty-five-minute period of work performance.

Our fictitious client then reports to the bank to deposit the tokens he has earned and to pay for lunch. Twenty tokens of his total earnings are taken so that he can attend lunch; the remaining number are placed in his account for safe keeping. He has now paid for the lunch period which will run from

11:50 A.M. until 12:30 P.M. Our client reports from lunch and punches in at 12:29 P.M. and reports to the work area supervisor and receives one token for being punctual. He then begins work on a blue level task of dust mopping that runs from 12:36 P.M. until 1:00 P.M. for which he earns two tokens and 100 percent. One o'clock until 1:30 P.M. finds our client performing the building services task of hand dusting. This task earns him a total of three tokens. The last thirty-minute period of the day finds our client performing another blue level task of hand sanding for which he earns another three tokens.

The end of the day will find all clients punching out on the time clock and reporting to the bank to receive tokens for punching the time clock at the correct time as well as punching the time clock without error. Our client receives eight tokens for having done all these behaviors correctly for the entire day. The supervisors of the areas to which our client reported will collect all the data obtained on this and all other clients and file this information in a central location by alphabetical order for all clients. These data are then collected by a verifier and reviewed with scrutiny to ascertain any errors made by supervisory personnel. When the verification is approved, this information is taken to the keypunch operator who punches the information directly onto IBM cards.

Figures 19 through 26 reflect our hypothetical client's performance for the day. The reader can refer to Chapter 8 for a view of these data in final computer form. This process is completed on each client daily with the assumption that routine and simplicity will guarantee accuracy in recording these data.

The reader should review this information with scrutiny to determine the actual procedures. The reader is also referred to Chapter 4, Figure 13 to verify percentages and amount of tokens earned.

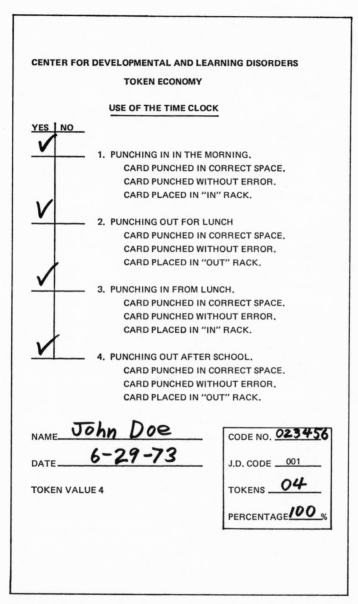

CENTER FOR DEVELOPMENTAL AND LEARNING DISORDERS

TOKEN ECONOMY

USE OF THE TIME CLOCK

YES | NO

1. PUNCHING IN IN THE MORNING.
   CARD PUNCHED IN CORRECT SPACE.
   CARD PUNCHED WITHOUT ERROR.
   CARD PLACED IN "IN" RACK.

2. PUNCHING OUT FOR LUNCH
   CARD PUNCHED IN CORRECT SPACE.
   CARD PUNCHED WITHOUT ERROR.
   CARD PLACED IN "OUT" RACK.

3. PUNCHING IN FROM LUNCH.
   CARD PUNCHED IN CORRECT SPACE.
   CARD PUNCHED WITHOUT ERROR.
   CARD PLACED IN "IN" RACK.

4. PUNCHING OUT AFTER SCHOOL.
   CARD PUNCHED IN CORRECT SPACE.
   CARD PUNCHED WITHOUT ERROR.
   CARD PLACED IN "OUT" RACK.

NAME *John Doe*

DATE *6-29-73*

TOKEN VALUE 4

CODE NO. *023456*

J.D. CODE *001*

TOKENS *04*

PERCENTAGE *100* %

Figure 19. John Doe's completed use of time clock job description for 6/29/73.

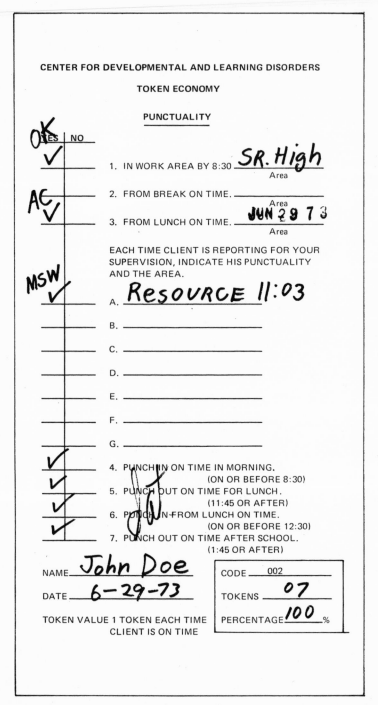

CENTER FOR DEVELOPMENTAL AND LEARNING DISORDERS

TOKEN ECONOMY

PUNCTUALITY

YES | NO

1. IN WORK AREA BY 8:30 ___SR. High___
   Area

2. FROM BREAK ON TIME. _____
   Area

3. FROM LUNCH ON TIME. __JUN 29 73__
   Area

EACH TIME CLIENT IS REPORTING FOR YOUR
SUPERVISION, INDICATE HIS PUNCTUALITY
AND THE AREA.

A. ___RESOURCE 11:03___

B. _____

C. _____

D. _____

E. _____

F. _____

G. _____

4. PUNCH IN ON TIME IN MORNING.
   (ON OR BEFORE 8:30)

5. PUNCH OUT ON TIME FOR LUNCH.
   (11:45 OR AFTER)

6. PUNCH IN FROM LUNCH ON TIME.
   (ON OR BEFORE 12:30)

7. PUNCH OUT ON TIME AFTER SCHOOL.
   (1:45 OR AFTER)

NAME __John Doe__

DATE __6-29-73__

CODE ___002___

TOKENS ___07___

PERCENTAGE ___100___%

TOKEN VALUE 1 TOKEN EACH TIME
CLIENT IS ON TIME

Figure 20. John Doe's completed punctuality job description for 6/29/73.

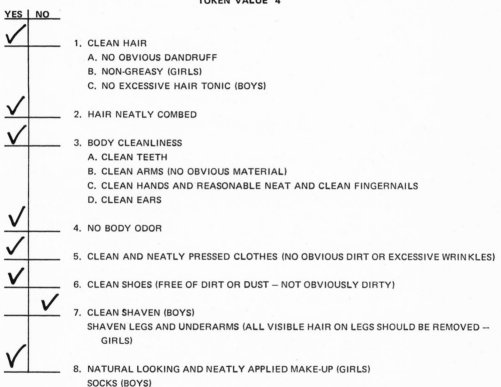

CENTER FOR DEVELOPMENTAL AND LEARNING DISORDERS

TOKEN ECONOMY

2-9-72

NAME **John Doe**

DATE **6-29-73**

GROOMING

TOKEN VALUE 4

YES	NO	
✓		1. CLEAN HAIR A. NO OBVIOUS DANDRUFF B. NON-GREASY (GIRLS) C. NO EXCESSIVE HAIR TONIC (BOYS)
✓		2. HAIR NEATLY COMBED
✓		3. BODY CLEANLINESS A. CLEAN TEETH B. CLEAN ARMS (NO OBVIOUS MATERIAL) C. CLEAN HANDS AND REASONABLE NEAT AND CLEAN FINGERNAILS D. CLEAN EARS
✓		4. NO BODY ODOR
✓		5. CLEAN AND NEATLY PRESSED CLOTHES (NO OBVIOUS DIRT OR EXCESSIVE WRINKLES)
✓		6. CLEAN SHOES (FREE OF DIRT OR DUST – NOT OBVIOUSLY DIRTY)
	✓	7. CLEAN SHAVEN (BOYS) SHAVEN LEGS AND UNDERARMS (ALL VISIBLE HAIR ON LEGS SHOULD BE REMOVED – GIRLS)
✓		8. NATURAL LOOKING AND NEATLY APPLIED MAKE-UP (GIRLS) SOCKS (BOYS)

CODE _____ 003 _____

TOKENS _____ **03** _____

PERCENTAGE _____ **087** _____ %

Figure 21. John Doe's completed grooming job description for 6/29/73.

CENTER FOR DEVELOPMENTAL AND LEARNING DISORDERS
TOKEN ECONOMY

1-21-72

NAME John Doe

DATE 6-29-73

SR. HIGH CLASS
CURRENT EVENTS
TOKEN VALUE 2

YES	NO
✓	

TWO (2) TOKENS FOR THREE (3) NEWSPAPER CLIPPINGS.

CODE 196

TOKENS 02

PERCENTAGE 100 %

READING
TOKEN VALUE 1 - 5
TIME 30 MINUTES
CODES 198 - 221

YES 1	2	3	4	5	6	7	NO 1	2	3	4	5	6	7
■													
	■												

1. 1 - 4 PAGES IN 30 MIN. - 1 TOKEN
2. 5 PAGES IN 30 MINUTES - 2 TOKENS
3. 10 PAGES IN 30 MINUTES- 3 TOKENS
4. 15 PAGES IN 30 MINUTES- 4 TOKENS
5. 20 PAGES IN 30 MINUTES- 5 TOKENS

CODE 208

TOKENS 06

PERCENTAGE 060 %

MATH
TOKEN VALUE 1 - 5
TIME 30 MINUTES
CODES 250 - 263

YES 1	2	3	4	5	6	7	NO 1	2	3	4	5	6	7
		■											
			■										

1. 1 - 4 PROBLEMS IN 30 MIN. - 1 TOKEN
2. 5 PROBLEMS IN 30 MINUTES - 2 TOKENS
3. 10 PROBLEMS IN 30 MINUTES - 3 TOKENS
4. 15 PROBLEMS IN 30 MINUTES - 4 TOKENS
5. 20 PROBLEMS IN 30 MINUTES - 5 TOKENS

CODE 254

TOKENS 03

PERCENTAGE 030 %

Figure 22. John Doe's completed academic job description for current events, reading, and math on 6/29/73.

CENTER FOR DEVELOPMENTAL AND LEARNING DISORDERS

TOKEN ECONOMY

NAME _John Doe_

9/8/71

DATE _6 – 29 – 73_

RESOURCE ROOM

DUKANE — AVID RECORDS

TOKEN VALUE 1 - 5

TIME 30 MINUTES

YES	NO		
		1.	0 – 30% – 1 TOKEN
✓		2.	31 – 70% – 2 TOKENS
		3.	71 – 80% – 3 TOKENS
		4.	81 – 90% – 4 TOKENS
		5.	91 – 100% – 5 TOKENS

CODE _____ 014 _____

TOKENS _____ *03* _____

PERCENTAGE _____ *080* _%

HOFFMAN

TOKEN VALUE 1 - 5

TIME 30 MINUTES

YES	NO		
		1.	0 – 30% – 1 TOKEN
✓		2.	31 – 70% – 2 TOKENS
		3.	71 – 80% – 3 TOKENS
		4.	81 – 90% – 4 TOKENS
		5.	91 – 100% – 5 TOKENS

CODE _____ 016 _____

TOKENS _____ *02* _____

PERCENTAGE _____ *050* _%

AVIDESK

TOKEN VALUE 1 - 5

YES	NO		
		1.	0 – 30% – 1 TOKEN
		2.	31 – 70% – 2 TOKENS
		3.	71 – 80% – 3 TOKENS
		4.	81 – 90% – 4 TOKENS
		5.	91 – 100% – 5 TOKENS

CODE _____ 013 _____

TOKENS _____

PERCENTAGE _____%

Figure 23. John Doe's completed resource room job description for 6/29/73.

DUST MOPPING - TOKEN VALUE 2

NAME **John Doe**

DATE **6-29-73**

YES	NO	
✓		1. ASSEMBLE MATERIALS: DUST MOPPING TOOL DUST MOP COVER PUTTY KNIFE COUNTER BRUSH DUST PAN
✓		2. PROCEED TO WORK AREA. TRAVEL TO WORK AREA ON THE RIGHT SIDE OF THE HALL.
✓		3. USING A FIGURE "8" MOTION, SWEEP ENTIRE AREA — DO NOT LIFT DUST MOP.
✓		4. USING COUNTER BRUSH, SWEEP DUST INTO DUST PAN.
✓		5. SWEEP ALL HARD-TO-REACH CORNERS WITH COUNTER BRUSH.
✓		6. REMOVE ALL CHEWING GUM AND OTHER GUMMY SUBSTANCES WITH PUTTY KNIFE (BEING CAREFUL NOT TO CUT FLOOR)
✓		7. SHAKE COUNTER BRUSH AND SWEEPING TOOL OVER THE NEAREST LARGE TRASH CONTAINER.
✓		8. RETURN SWEEPING TOOL & SUPPLIES TO SUPPLY ROOM AND PLACE AGAINST THE WALL.
✓		9. CLEAN DUST PAN AND COUNTER BRUSH WITHOUT USING WATER ON COUNTER BRUSH.
✓		10. INFORM SUPERVISOR WHEN TASK IS COMPLETED.

EXCESSIVE TALKING - NO. TIMES _____

LEAVING WORK AREA - NO. TIMES _____

IDLE - NUMBER TIMES _____

TIME FINISHED **29 Jun P 1:00**

TIME STARTED **29 Jun P 12:36**

TIME WORKED **24 min**

AREA ASSIGNED **5ᵗʰ floor**

CODE	124
TOTAL TOKENS	**02**
PERCENTAGE	**100** %

Figure 24. John Doe's completed dust mopping job description for 6/29/73.

CENTER FOR DEVELOPMENTAL AND LEARNING DISORDERS

TOKEN ECONOMY

HAND DUSTING — TOKEN VALUE 4

NAME **John Doe**

WORK AREA **Work SamplE Room**

DATE **6-29-73**

YES	NO	
✓		1. ASSEMBLE SUPPLIES. A. DUST RAGS (CLEAN)
✓		2. DUST ALL PLACES THAT YOU CAN REACH. (NOT WALLS OR FLOORS)
✓		3. USE A NEW RAG FOR EACH ROOM OR HALL TO BE DUSTED.
	✓	4. PLACE RAGS IN TRASH CAN WHEN YOU MOVE TO NEXT ROOM.
✓		5. INFORM SUPERVISOR WHEN JOB IS COMPLETED

EXCESSIVE TALKING - NO. TIMES _____

LEAVING WORK AREA - NO. TIMES _____

IDLE - NUMBER TIMES _____

TIME FINISHED **29 Jun P 1:30**

TIME STARTED **29 Jun P 1:00**

TIME WORKED **30 Min**

CODE	136
TOTAL TOKENS	**03**
PERCENTAGE	**080** %

Figure 25. John Doe's completed hand dusting job description for 6/29/73.

CENTER FOR DEVELOPMENTAL AND LEARNING DISORDERS

TOKEN ECONOMY

10-13-72

NAME *John Doe*

DATE *6-29-73*

HAND SANDING

TOKEN VALUE 3 per ½ hour

YES	NO	
✓		1. SELECT PROPER GRIT PAPER.
✓		2. PLACE WOOD IN A FIXED POSITION.
✓		3. PROCEED TO SAND USING GENTLE PRESSURE FOLLOWING GRAIN.
✓		4. PUSH SAND PAPER EVENLY ACROSS OBJECT.
✓		5. DISCARD USED SAND PAPER, REPLACE USABLE SANDPAPER IN DESIGNATED PLACE.
✓		6. REPLACE WOOD IN PROPER PLACE.
✓		7. CLEAN UP WORK AREA.
✓		8. INFORM SUPERVISOR WHEN TASK IS FINISHED

WORKS AT A STEADY PACE:
    EXCESSIVE TALKING - NO. TIMES _____
    LEAVING WORK AREA - NO. TIMES _____
    IDLE - NUMBER TIMES _____

TIME FINISHED 29 Jun 1:58

TIME STARTED 29 Jun 1:32

TOTAL TIME *26 min*

CODE	114
TOKENS	*03*
PERCENTAGE	*100* %

Figure 26. John Doe's completed hand sanding job description for 6/29/73.

CHAPTER 7

INDIVIDUALIZATION OF ECONOMY PROCESS

FOR SPECIFIC CASES

THE TOKEN ECONOMY is not an end product and does not operate in exactly the same way as does society. This system is nothing more than a treatment process which has the terminal goal of adjusting the handicapped person to society. The objectivity and persistent adherence to the operant conditioning theory as well as the mechanistic appearance of this approach has precipitated the criticism that such approaches are not humanistic in nature. The humanist would view the token economy as being the producer of mercenary robots who follow the incentive of a token as a horse would follow a carrot.

The humanist's point is well-taken; however, attention should be called to the point most often overlooked by critics. The primary defense of such a program is that it is totally individualized. Concern is with the individual and not with groups of individuals as is the case with traditional approaches to Rehabilitation. A behavioral approach stresses very strongly the utilization of praise and supervisor contact with the client. This contact assures that the client is not lost in the shuffle of the group, but that his supervisor is genuinely concerned about him and his improvements.

A close look at the program will reveal that the clients are not forced into compliance by a hideous creature known as a token. The element of human choice remains. The job description for grooming does not say that a person will not have any facial hair. It in essence says, "If you do not have facial hair, you will receive a token." The client is to make the choice between a mustache and a token and if the mustache is higher ranked within his value system, he will more than likely choose to wear a mustache. The loss of the one token should not be that harmful in that he can earn approximately forty-five tokens per day. Also, the system is so arranged as to allow the client to work harder on some other task in order to regain the lost token.

The humanist would view the token as a bribe to get a client to perform behaviors consistent with the program philosophy. He might disagree with bribery as a practice and disagree with having to pay for behavior that the client should do without receiving payment. The above train of thought overlooks the fact that a bribe is something given with the extraction of a promise from the client that a particular behavior will be done at a later time. Such a procedure would then reinforce the client's deceitful behavior if the task for which he received the bribe was not performed. Waiting for the behavior to occur and then giving remuneration for a task well-done is an entirely different concept. This concept is called *contingent positive reinforcement* which strengthens the behavior or the frequency of occurrence of the behavior and lends itself to the fading process mentioned in previous chapters.

The fading concept allows a gradual removal of the amount or frequency of the remuneration so the client can perform the desired behavior without receiving pay for doing what he is supposed to do anyway. The client must learn through some process what he should and should not do; this process is an efficient procedure for doing just that.

An example of fading in relation to the open token economy would be the removal of steps that the client has mastered on a particular job description and having the client perform these removed steps without remuneration. A job description for wood staining can be offered as an example. A client can be performing steps six, seven and eight of this job perfectly but have an inconsistent performance on the remaining steps. The supervisor merely marks out with a felt tip marker steps six, seven and eight as shown in Figure 27. This description automatically becomes a six-step job and correctly performed steps are now being performed without receiving tokens for accurately completing the three steps. Hopefully, the entire description would be marked in this manner until each step can be performed without pay for having done what he should have been able to do anyway.

As the system is arranged, it is a function of employer and society demands, not a function of the desires and wishes of the personnel who operate the program. Criteria for success on the job description are a function of employer requirements; the need for improved reading skills is a function of the symbolic language established by society; and the need to operate an automobile is a function of not having an adequate transit system. When at all possible the token economy is structured as a teaching device; the more the client learns, the more the economy process relies on society's control and less on the artificially structured economy system.

In many cases the token economy system is more humanistic than the prevailing rehabilitation system. A behavioral approach has the basic philosophy that if achievement and improvement is not noted in the client's behavior, this failure to respond is the fault of the program and not the fault of the client. Where traditional programs view misbehavior and malconduct as grounds for dismissal or termination from the program, a behavioral system views the occurrence of such behaviors as being a function of the program's inability to identify relevant work tasks or reinforcing stimuli which the client will work to obtain. Where a traditional approach views appropriate behavior as the responsibility of the client, a behavioral ap-

CENTER FOR DEVELOPMENTAL AND LEARNING DISORDERS

TOKEN ECONOMY

4-3-72

NAME_____

DATE_____

STAINING

TOKEN VALUE 3 per ½ hour

YES | NO

_____ 1. SELECT PROPER STAIN.

_____ 2. SELECT CLEAN RAGS OR BRUSH.

_____ 3. SELECT AND INSPECT WOOD FOR NICKS, CUTS, AND SCRATCHES.

_____ 4. START STAINING WITH SHORT STROKES FOLLOWING WOOD GRAIN.

_____ 5. APPLY EVENLY TO SURFACE.

_____ 6. DISCARD RAGS OR CLEAN UP BRUSHES.

_____ 7. CLEAN WORK AREA.

_____ 8. REPLACE TOOLS.

_____ 9. INFORM SUPERVISOR WHEN JOB IS COMPLETED.

WORKS AT A STEADY PACE:
EXCESSIVE TALKING - NO. TIMES_____
LEAVING WORK AREA - NO. TIMES_____
IDLE - NUMBER TIMES_____

TIME FINISHED_____

TIME STARTED_____

TOTAL TIME_____

CODE_____151_____

TOKENS_____

PERCENTAGE_____%

Figure 27. An example of the concept of *fading* on the token economy job description.

proach views responsibility as a learned concept and teaches behaviors which are associated with the construct of responsibility. Viewing rehabilitation as a learning process on the part of the client puts a new prospective on the traditional job training process and removes the assumptions that the client should be cooperative, responsible, diligent and purposeful in his actions before he can be rehabilitated.

The alternative to not using an incentive system is to use a punishment system. The punishment system does not necessarily imply corporal punishment, but more subtle forms of punishment such as reduction in the amount of a maintenance and transportation check which might be provided to the client in order for him to participate in the program or the withholding of preferred activities because of failure to follow the dictates of the program. Further malconduct in a traditional approach would precipitate expulsion from the program and denial of rehabilitation services as a function of misconduct. The behavioral approach could eliminate these problems to a very large degree by attempting to teach the concept of cooperativeness by the same step-wise fashion as is done with teaching a specific job skill. Many points of the behavioral approach are more humanistic than would be the alternative to a behavioral approach.

The individualization of the economy is the most important and workable concept of the entire system. A client can be treated differently from all other clients yet be treated the same as all other clients. An illustration of this procedure is the point system.

THE POINT SYSTEM

The point system is merely another application of the same underlying principles of the operant paradigm. This process can be used as a fading procedure or halfway arrangement for the token economy system to the economic system established by society.

The economy can become an elementary procedure for a client who has been in the program for a couple of years and has seen numerous friends employed. He may see much younger clients taking over red level jobs which were his and his peers' domain for quite a while; and he may amass a large bank account of tokens, making the earning of more seem irrelevant.

The occurrence of this problem is of paramount concern to the program because this client has not met criterion on a number of items, yet he is well beyond criterion on most job descriptions.

The point system has become a convenient procedure to help alleviate this dilemma. The client may be taken off the economy so that he can now look back at the younger group with the smugness that he is one step closer to employment. His behavior, which is not yet up to criterion, can still be made contingent; the behaviors which are above criterion can be dropped

CENTER FOR DEVELOPMENTAL AND LEARNING DISORDERS

TOKEN ECONOMY

NAME———————— John Doe ————————————

DATE ————————————————————————

CODE ———— JD 023456 ————————

ACTIVITY	POSSIBLE POINTS	PERCENTAGE	TOTAL POINTS
TIME CLOCK 001	30		
PUNCTUALITY 002	30		
GROOMING 003	30		
WORK ACTIVITY	60		
TOTAL	150		

Figure 28. An example of the daily point system recording device.

from his earning repertoire. All reinforcement can be made contingent upon the below criterion behaviors making the amount of reinforcement high for each deficit category. All reinforcement at this point can become money which is a closer simulation of the real world. When the criterion is met on the behaviors outlined on the point system, the client may be referred for placement.

An example of the point system may be a client who is being trained for a specific job such as mail clerk and office boy in a large building. He may work satisfactorily; however, he does not punch the time clock adequately, nor is he punctual or properly groomed. The point system could make these three behaviors constitute three fifths of his earning power with his work activity counting as only two fifths of his total possible points. Figure 28 shows how this procedure would allow all behaviors to fit onto one job description for the day and percentages and total points figured for each day. The job descriptions are still individually checked by the supervisor; however, the client has little contact with them. The client's total concern is with the one sheet for the total day's performance. He is no longer paid on the completion of a job or for every thirty minutes, but accumulates points and is paid money at the week's end. This fading procedure helps immensely in the transition from token economy to actual job placement.

The client is also counseled at this point to advise him of his needs before he is placed on a job. His performance in each of the areas listed on the point sheet is discussed in detail, and the level of success needed before he begins job interviews is also discussed. The client's schedule is changed so as to refer him to a resource classroom to receive instruction in filling out job applications, learning how to conduct himself in the job interview, and to observe occupational tapes in the area for which he and the program are considering employment.

The point system can easily be implemented with the use of a *Work Request* form. The *Work Request* form is written on red paper and in generally the same style as the job description. It becomes a convenient recording device when only general directions for completion of a task are required. This device assists in the fading process in that the behavioral objectives have been eliminated, and standards on the job requests are made (See Appendix C) .

This procedure is helpful as part of the program, but what about after-school hours and minor home problems? The answer to this problem is the contingency contract.

CONTINGENCY CONTRACT

Case History

Tom was a twelve-year-old clinical referral who was experiencing academic difficulties in reading and mathematics. Tom's parents are both college graduates and have difficulty understanding the scholastic difficulties of Tom and his two older brothers. Tom has continually had difficulty in school, having repeated the first grade and transferred from school to school to determine the most acceptable placement for him. Because of Tom's embarrassment he had begun to refuse to answer questions in class and to otherwise cover up his lack of ability.

Tom's mother reports that adjustment in school is quite good and that he does not present a major discipline problem. They do have some difficulty in disciplining him at home in terms of getting him to finish his schoolwork and carry out various chores. In the past his father has not spent very much time with Tom, but he is trying to arrange his schedule to be able to do this now. Tom does not have many friends and enjoys being outside and building things.

The Wechsler Intelligence Scale for Children demonstrated that he obtained a verbal IQ of 89, a performance IQ of 117, and a full scale IQ of 102. This discrepancy between verbal and performance IQ is most remarkable. His lowest subtest score was on general information in which he functioned more like a seven-year-old. His general vocabulary and concept formation also fell quite low.

On the performance test he performed at the bright normal to superior range. Generally, this type of test performance is found in children who have come from a lower socioeconomic environment. Tom does not reflect this kind of background, and one can only conjecture that this difficulty is based on random genetic causes. A picture vocabulary test gave a mental age of twelve years and three months which would place him in the average range of intelligence.

An achievement test was given and he obtained a reading grade placement of 5.2, spelling grade placement of 1.9, and arithmetic grade placement of 4.5. His spelling performance was quite remarkable as compared with his reading and arithmetic scores. He demonstrated a lack of effective word attack methods, including phonics. For example, he spelled circle *cirle,* round was spelled *rund,* and lecturer was spelled *letartur.* It is quite likely that his auditory discrimination and auditory memory are also quite poor.

The psychological summary indicated that Tom will continue to present major difficulties in school. With this type of school achievement, much of the sixth grade curriculum will be beyond his ability.

The father was surprised to know that his son was achieving so poorly, particularly in spelling. It was pointed out to him and the mother that Tom presented a great deal more ability in the performance area than in areas involving language. The prereading information, along with Tom's lack of motivation to do academics, was discussed with the parents and the suggestion of a contingency contract was made.

The parents were asked to report the behaviors which were most disturbing in relation to Tom. They were listed as taking a bath, homework, classroom participations, and conservation of home expenses. The parents were also asked to determine in a hierarchical arrangement the things or activities which Tom would work to obtain and the things he would work to avoid. After completion of the information an explanation was given the parents which was an outline of the procedures of the contract. Complete and total assurance was obtained from the parents that the contract would be followed as written. Deviations from the contract would be cleared by the authors before being included in the contractual agreement.

The following contingency contract was written for Tom and his parents. This contract included tutoring that would be conducted by the authors on an outpatient basis. This arrangement could or would allow treatment even though Tom's problem could not be categorized as one which would allow enrollment in the token economy program.

The Contingency Contract

The following is an outline of how Tom may earn points which may be traded for rewards or pleasurable activities. Tom may earn points in five different ways: (1) by taking a bath, (2) homework checked at home, (3) homework checked at school, (4) classroom participation checked at school, and (5) by being tutored. Points earned will be as listed on the points earned sheet accompanying this contract (See Figure 29). Points spent will

EARNING POINTS

WEEK ———

	Monday	Tuesday	Wednesday	Thursday	Friday	Weekend
Taking a bath — without parent telling him to do so — 10 points with parent telling once — 5 points with parent telling twice — 0 points						
Homework Checked at Home neatly completed as assigned — 10 points 3/4 completed — 5 points 1/2 completed — 2 points 1/4 completed — 0 points						
Homework Checked at School Letter grade A — 10 points Letter grade B — 5 points Letter grace C — 2 points Letter grade D — 0 points						
Classroom participation participated 4 times — 10 points participated 3 times — 5 points participated 2 times — 3 points participated 1 time — 1 point						
Tutoring Improved in amount read and Less errors — 10 points Improved in Less errors — 5 points Improved in amount read — 3 points No improvement — 0 points						
Bonus of 20 points for perfect day.						

Figure 29. The recording device for Tom's parents to record his daily earnings by category.

SPENDING POINTS

	Monday	Tuesday	Wednesday	Thursday	Friday	Weekend	Total
Money 1¢ per point							
Special Outings −(20 points per outing) 　1. football game 　2. going to movie 　3. going to the drugstore 　4. driving car at farm 　5. 22 shells at farm 　6. boating at farm 　7. playing golf 　8. golf lessons 　9. carpet golf 　10. bowling							
T.V. Time − 5 points per hour Other home entertainment at same rate.							
Outside Activities 3 points per hour playing with friend (until 6 o'clock)							
Drawing or Reading cost 1 point per hour							
TOTAL							

Figure 30. The recording device for Tom's parents to record his spending by day and category.

cost as listed on the spending point sheet accompanying this contract (See Figure 30). A perfect week in which all points are earned will yield Tom a bonus of fifty points which may be spent at any time.

In the event that Tom wants to participate in some activity and he does not have enough points to do so, then he must remain in his room without any type of entertainment until the opportunity for earning more points arises. This will usually take the form of having to retire early rather than watching television.

Accompanying the family on family outings requires no spending of points if the entire family is required to go. Trips to the farm will cost Tom nothing; however, activities at the farm will cost as if he were at home. If Tom has enough points to do an activity that he himself chooses, this activity may not be refused him. An example may be that he wishes to attend a movie on Friday night and has ample points to both attend and pay for the cost of the movie. Provisions will then be made for him to attend. However, the type of movie seen may still be limited by the parents. Points may not be spent during homework time nor during school or tutoring time.

Immediately upon return from school, Tom will begin his homework assignment as indicated by his teacher on the homework assignment sheet (See Figure 31). He will also give his parents the homework sheet checked by the teacher for the previous day and receive his points for doing so. Also,

DAILY TEACHER REPORT

DATE_____   FOR_____

SUBJECT	HOMEWORK GRADE ON LAST NIGHTS	CLASSROOM PARTICIPATION GRADE FOR DAY	INITIAL IN INK
	AVG._____ AVG._____		

HOMEWORK ASSIGNMENTS:

_____

_____

_____

_____

_____

_____

_____

_____

Figure 31. The chart which was completed by each of Tom's teachers which reflected the behaviors for which Tom obtained points issued by his parents.

his classroom participation sheet will yield him points earned. He will work on his homework until it is completed and has been checked by his mother. Upon completing this task his points will be paid and recorded on the points earned sheet.

Weekend activities are usually exempt from the contract except in the case of special outings as identified on the point spending sheet. Tom may also earn bonus points from his tutoring activities on Tuesday and Thursday when an exceptional job is noted by the tutor.

Tom will no longer receive an allowance. His allowance will be earned by the point system and he may, if he wishes, cash in his entire earnings for money which could be approximately five dollars per week.

If Tom remains after school for special help classes, these special help clasess will yield him five points for each attendance. It is agreed by both the Contractor (Tom's parents) and the Contractee (Tom) that this contract will be strictly adhered to. Particular points of legality which present difficulty in interpretation will be checked for interpretation with the authors of this contract.

Particular family requirements of Tom will still remain in effect, and Tom may receive bonus payments for these activities. For example, the making of his bed, the turning out of light switches or other routine chores may be rewarded; however, these are not to exceed twenty-five points per week.

Complete and accurate records of points earned and points spent will be kept by the Contractors and returned to the authors of the contract on a weekly basis. These points will be totaled and plotted on a graph weekly to note the amount of progress demonstrated by Tom (See Figure 32).

Signed before a witness as of the indicated date.

	Date
Contractor, Mr.	
	Date
Contractor, Mrs.	
	Date
Contractee, Tom	
	Date
Witness	

Results of Contract

Tom's progress from a five-day baseline period encompasses one week and this time is identified in Figure 32. The contract was terminated during Christmas holidays to aid in the fading or gradual decline of the requirements of the contract. Allowance and other rewards were maintained as being contingent upon appropriate behaviors; however, the points no longer have to be calculated.

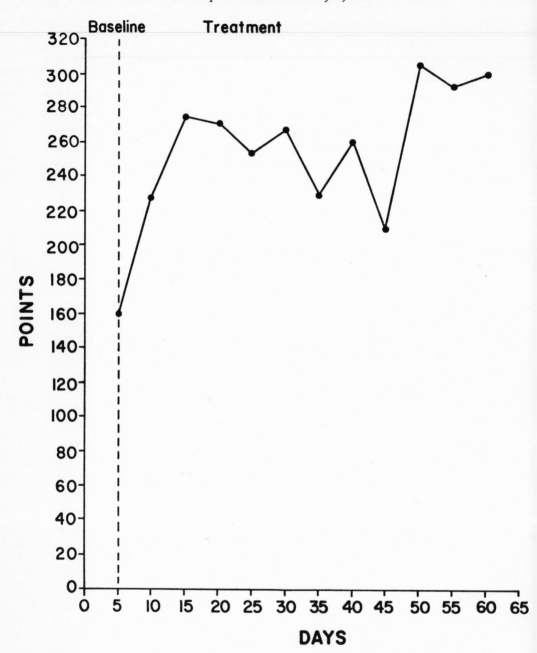

Figure 32. Tom's performance on baseline and eleven 5-day periods of treatment.

This procedure offered an excellent opportunity to control maladaptive behaviors within the home without the author's presence. This device can be extremely helpful when used in combination with the open token economy system as a supplement to a client's treatment procedure. This process can work equally well in the absence of the token economy. Further discussion of contingency contracting is available and should be consulted before attempting this procedure (Cantrell, *et al.*, 1969; Homme, 1966; Welch, 1970).

SUMMARY

These are only a few of the special applications which can be made under the confines of the open token economy. The numerous amendments to the standard procedure are only a function of the supervisor's innovation, strict adherence to a behavioral philosophy and genuine concern for client improvement to the point of employment.

Other subsystems are the use of charts on the wall to record appropriate behavior and give special praise for a job well-done. The use of contingent praise and bonus free time may all be used with the open token economy system with no detrimental effect on the overall program.

CHAPTER 8

THE USE OF RECORDED INFORMATION

U NDER THE AUSPICES of a behavior modification paradigm it is extremely important to adhere dogmatically to an accepted behavioral experimental design. The express purpose of the program outlined for your consideration is not one which would stress the utilization of a research procedure for a service function rendered to clients. Data have to be collected not for research proof but for assurance of accurate collection. There is a substantial reservoir of data which has been accumulated from primarily the past ten years which reflects that operant conditioning paradigms work effectively when the appropriate rules governing treatment procedures are strictly adhered to.

These data reveal that the behavioral approach to treatment of deviant behaviors is one of the most practical and expeditious treatment procedures available for working with the handicapped population. The justification for use of this method is already in the literature, and further discussion of the merit of operant conditioning procedures with the handicapped is purely pedantic. However, if one follows operant conditioning theory to the letter, data collection will occur and use of these data for program improvement is assured. The use of the data then is not for program proof but for assurance that operant conditioning rules and appropriate treatment procedures are followed.

In a program which is designed primarily to render a service to a handicapped population, each individual becomes a point of interest, not the entire program. The open token economy system is designed primarily for this purpose.

DIAGNOSTIC PROFILE

The data which were collected on our hypothetical client in Chapter 6 were done to analyze the effects the program had on this one client's work and work-related behaviors. The collected information over time, when graphed, mirrors a diagnostic profile of the effects of program treatment. Analysis of this graphic information becomes feedback to program personnel as to the adequacy of their attempts to modify the client's behavior to more adequately approximate real world expectancies. For example, the graphic display of a client's performance in all program areas demonstrates a higher rate of performance on all job descriptions except those related to auxiliary work behaviors of grooming and punctuality.

The client could receive a restructuring of treatment, making more re-inforcement contingent upon improvement in these two areas. When this treatment is instituted, the graphs can subsequently be re-evaluated to determine the effectiveness of the new treatment procedure. A rise in the performance rate would reflect that the treatment procedure was appropriate and a drop in the performance rate would suggest trying another approach to solving the problem. Such a procedure could continue until an adequate rise is noted in all percentages.

The above system ensures that program personnel are dispensing adequate treatment. The graphic interpretation can save enormous amounts of time and effort on the part of the program personnel. Without this information there is no assurance that the treatment being given a client is adequately remediating the inappropriate behavior. This diagnostic approach removes the question of adequacy of treatment by graphically representing the effects of treatment over time.

PROGRAM REFERRAL FOR PLACEMENT

When appropriate criteria percentages are reached on auxiliary work behaviors and appropriately assigned job descriptions reflect a high rate of responding on red level jobs, a referral can be made for placement. This referral can be to a person who is in charge of client placement, to a voca-tional rehabilitation counselor, or even directly to the employer. Job family areas can be recommended as employment possibilities for clients based on performances of related job assignments as diagnostically interpreted by staff from the graphs of performances.

The data obtained on clients can be utilized as a predictor of job success. That is, the utilization of this system of rehabilitation could establish definite criteria in the form of percentage levels which would become adequate predictors of job success. The successfully employed clients could easily be compared with those clients who attempted employment and failed. The diagnostic profile of each success and failure could determine areas of strength and weaknesses of the system as it related to specific jobs.

A procedure could be established whereby program personnel do job analysis of available jobs within the community to ascertain specific indices of requirements for the completion of that job. These measures could then be incorporated in the construction of the job description to ensure that the success criterion is an adequate predictor of success at that particular job. An example of this procedure could be the utilization of 6 cycle paper (available through Behavioral Research Company) to determine the rate at which a job is performed within an assembly plant. The rate could then be incorporated as a success criterion on assembly job descriptions within the program. Such a procedure would greatly facilitate efforts to make the job description an adequate predictor of job success.

DATA AND THE REHABILITATION PROCESS

The graphic information obtained on clients becomes a true refinement of the rehabilitation of the client. The discussion in Chapter 1 of traditional procedures of evaluation, adjustment and training can be vastly improved by the utilization of the open token economy system.

Evaluation, adjustment and training become intermeshed in this system. The client is evaluated daily on every type of job for which the program has a job description in order to determine areas of greatest proficiency. While in the process of being evaluated, his behavior is also being adjusted toward approximations of normal work behavior; that is, he is becoming well-groomed by earning tokens for appropriate changes in his appearance; he is becoming punctual by following the punctuality job description and receiving appropriate reward for doing so; and he is becoming academically proficient as a function of his receiving reinforcement for approximations to his terminal academic goal. The client is trained in particular jobs by repeated applications of job descriptions which reveal a substandard performance, and he is given contingent reinforcement for noted improvements in his performance.

The combination of evaluation, adjustment and training make for a more efficient rehabilitation program. The entire program works as a single unit in order to improve behavior on the part of clients so that the client is performing to such a degree that job placement is possible.

Data Collection

All information has to be collected systematically so as to minimize error and prevent data backlog. A program with fifty active clients will be swamped with data within a week's time unless a convenient data collection, collation, storage and retrieval system is organized. It is not only a convenient procedure, but a necessity for smooth operation of the economy.

The Most Productive Way

The computer will eliminate numerous problems associated with maintaining daily banking information as well as the graph plotting procedures. The daily banking information (such as depositing and spending) must be tabulated daily so the client knows at all times his balance of tokens on deposit. The graphs for each client must be plotted monthly for staff information.

The collection of daily data for the economy would consist of two major elements: the client's punctuality card and the job descriptions of the client's work for the day. This information should be placed in a central location by an established time.

The punctuality cards and use of the time clock job description should be collected during the afternoon check-out at the bank, after which the percentages for punctuality during the day are completed. The cards are collated and the client's computer code is written on the card.

This computer code has been mentioned previously in Chapter 4. The data retrieval box consists of this code, the tokens earned, and the percentage as discussed also in Chapter 4 (See Figure 3, Section D).

All job descriptions have a three-digit code for computer processing beginning with 001 through 999. This allows for 999 coded descriptions (See Figure 33). Caution should be taken not to change description codes because once data have been stored under that number, the computer cannot distinguish between names, it only reads numbers. If a job description is retired because it is obsolete or for any other reason, that three-digit code should not be used again. When establishing a system of this type one should project how many codes the program would use until it is dissolved, otherwise the computer program would have to be rewritten.

Codes can be assigned to job descriptions so staff can easily recognize frequently used ones without referring to a chart. For example, use of the time clock, punctuality and grooming are completed on every client each day. These are coded 001, 002 and 003 respectively. The codes for Sullivan Programmed Reading Series were selected for easy reference to the book in which the client is reading. For example, code 201 is book one, code 202 is book two, and so on through book twenty-one which is coded 221. Caution should be taken not to initiate use of new job descriptions until properly coded.

Each client has a six-digit code preceded by his initials. This six-digit code is his rehabilitation case number if one has been assigned. It could be his social security number or any digital numbering system. The use of the time clock job description reveals an extra space in the data retrieval box entitled *Code No.* (Figure 34). The client's six-digit code is written here for keypunching at the end of the day. This code will identify all job description percentages and tokens earned for the day for that client.

Job descriptions used in each department for the day are deposited alphabetically in a daily file. The use of the time clock and punctuality card job descriptions are then deposited in the daily file from the bank. All job descriptions for the day for each client are then collated in a sequence which facilitates the keypunching and programming of the data. For example, the use of the time clock and punctuality card job descriptions (codes 001 and 002) are placed on top of the grooming job description (code

CODE	JOB DESCRIPTION
001	Use of the Time Clock
002	Punctuality
003	Grooming
004	Tooth Brushing
005	Junior High Aide-Newspaper
006	Intermediate Class Teaching Aide - Arithmetic
007	Intermediate Teacher Aide - Morning
008	Intermediate Teacher Aide - Morning
009	Unit Time (Junior High Class)
010	Free Time (Junior High Class)
011	Driver Manual Workbook - Alabama Driving Handbook
012	Driver Education Workbook
013	Avidesk
014	Dukane
015	Sullivan Reading Test
016	Hoffman
017	Reading Flash Cards
018	Interview Tapes, Occupational Tapes
019	Programmed Primer
020	Bed Making
021	Cleaning Bathroom Lavatory
022	Cleaning Bathtub
023	Cleaning Blinds
024	Cleaning Hair Brushes
025	Cleaning Refrigerator
026	Cleaning Shower
027	Cleaning Sink
028	Cleaning Toilet
029	Cleaning Wall Tile
030	Folding Towels

999

Figure 33. The job description titles and computer code for jobs 001 through 999.

CODE NO. _____

J.D. CODE_____ 001 _____

TOKENS_____

PERCENTAGE _____ %

Figure 34. Data retrieval box located on lower right-hand corner of all job descriptions.

003). Other job descriptions are placed in numerical order according to code assignment (004, 005, etc.). The codes, percentages and tokens earned on all job descriptions are given a final check with necessary corrections. These data are then placed in alphabetical order by client name and key-punched onto IBM cards.

The data are stored on a daily basis. At regular intervals, usually every eight to ten weeks, the data are broken down into individual client records, computer graphs are printed, and the data stored permanently. This filing procedure allows for flexibility in data retrieval for case staffings and for handy reference of general information on client's current assignments and progress.

The efficient collation and storage of data is dependent upon the co-ordination and cooperation of all personnel involved. Two sources of po-tential difficulty in the handling and storage of these data are: (1) late or non-arrival of data at the collection point which would deter the flow of data into storage and increase the probability of data being misplaced or misfiled and (2) data which are insufficient or incorrect which can cause difficulty in charting the data for case staffings.

Computerization. Data from the original pilot group on the open token economy were hand plotted and only general behavioral categories were graphed. That is, all data on numerous job descriptions from self-help, work and auxiliary work assignments were plotted on one graph. The computer plots involved isolation of particular job descriptions to determine the behaviors in which a client may require improvement.

Recommended procedures used in collecting, keypunching and com-puter plotting the data are as follows:

1. All job descriptions should have a section that contains the job code, number of tokens paid and percentage of accuracy on the job description. This section should be completed in full on each description submitted.

2. Each client's job descriptions should be compiled on a daily basis, checked to ascertain that all data have been received, and filed in the client's data file.

3. Whenever there is a need for graphs for a particular client, his data are keypunched and processed on the computer. These data may also be hand plotted at this point.

4. The plots affixed by the computer to a graph format must have lines drawn connecting these plots. The graph lines must be identified as par-ticular job descriptions. Blue level jobs may be printed in blue ink, red level with red ink and green level job descriptions in green ink.

The process outlined here can be designed to provide a daily current bank balance and an up-to-date value for total tokens earned by an indi-vidual client. However, the program does not need to follow specifically

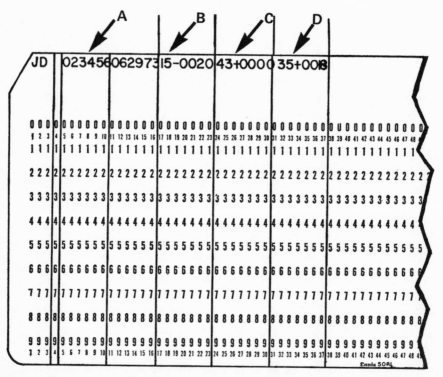

A	B	C	D
Col 1-3 I n i t i a l s	Col 5-10 Client Number	Col 11-16 Date 11-12 Mo. 13-14 Day 15-16 Yr.	Col 17-80 Code-amounts 17-18 Item or incentive code 19 + or − 20-23 Amount in tokens 24-25 Code 26 + or − 27-30 Amount Etc.

Figure 35. Data reduction for daily banking information on computer cards.

Figure 36. Analysis of this computer card can easily demonstrate a client's banking and spending patterns for the day without having to handle excessive amounts of paper.

the steps outlined here. The purpose of keypunching data is not only for computer use but for data reduction and storage as well.

The codes may be punched in the following manner for daily banking information: columns one through three are client's initials (Figure 35, Section A), columns five through ten are the client's rehabilitation case number (Figure 35, Section B), columns eleven through sixteen are the date (Figure 35, Section C) and columns seventeen through eighty contain the reinforcing contingency codes and amounts (Figure 35, Section D).

Figure 36 is a completed IBM card for a client's banking and spendings for the day. Columns one through three, five through ten and eleven through sixteen contain initials, client number and date respectively (Figure 36, Section A). Analysis of columns seventeen through twenty-three shows that this client went to lunch, classified 15 and paid twenty tokens by check, keypunched −0020 (Figure 36, Section B). Columns twenty-four through thirty are classified 43 for a canteen item. The +0000 code indicates he paid tokens rather than writing a check. To verify the amount spent you would have to look at the daily banking sheet (Figure 16, Chapter 5). This amount will not be deducted from his bank balance (Figure 36, Section C). Columns thirty-one through thirty-seven show a deposit, classified 35, of eighteen tokens, keypunched +0018 (Figure 36, Section D).

Cards as shown in Figure 36 are punched daily for each client in the program. These cards are put into a program setup as shown in Figure 37 and a daily banking sheet is run as shown in Figure 38.

The following procedure is illustrative of the reduction of data for the daily job description's code, tokens earned and percentages onto IBM cards.

Job, token and percentage cards are set up as shown in Figure 39. Columns one through three are client initials, columns five through ten are client number and columns eleven through sixteen are the date. Columns seventeen through eighty contain the job number, the tokens earned and the percentage level of functioning for each job assigned for the day.

Figure 40 is a completed IBM card for a client's auxiliary and work behaviors for the day. Columns one through three, five through ten and eleven through sixteen contain initials, client number and date respectively (Figure 40, Section A). Analysis of columns seventeen through twenty-four shows this client's use of the time clock behavior, code 001; he earned four tokens, keypunched 04 and functioned at a level of 100 percent, keypunched 100 (Figure 40, Section B). In columns twenty-five through thirty-two we see punctuality, code 002; he earned seven tokens, keypunched 07 and functioned at a level of 100 percent, keypunched 100 (Figure 40, Section C). His grooming, code 003, shows he earned three tokens, keypunched 03 and functioned at 87 percent, keypunched 087 (Figure 40, Section D). These are auxiliary work behaviors which all clients have recorded each day.

PROGRAM SETUP BANKING

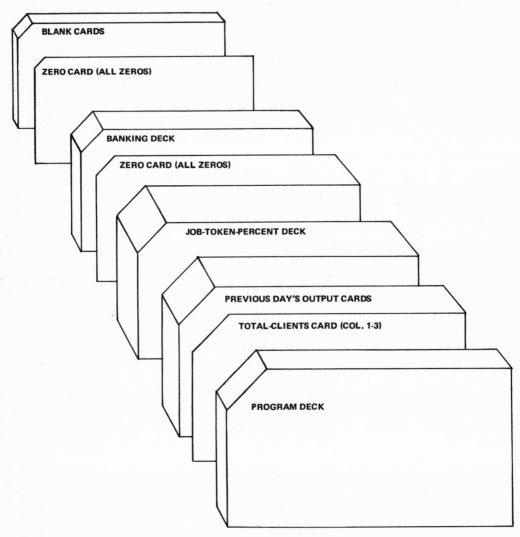

Figure 37. Computer program setup for daily banking information.

Academic job descriptions begin with column forty-one. Code 196 is current events and shows this client earned two tokens, keypunched 02. He functioned at 100 percent, keypunched 100 (Figure 40, Section E). He is reading in book 8, keypunched 208, for which his performance earned him six tokens, keypunched 06 and functioned at a level of 60 percent, keypunched 060.

He is working in book 4 of math, keypunched 254. He earned three

CENTER FOR DEVELOPMENTAL AND LEARNING DISORDERS
DIVISION OF SPECIAL EDUCATION AND VOCATIONAL REHABILITATION

DATE 7-15-71 CLIENT NUM.	TOKEN ECONOMY TOTAL TOKENS EARNED	CURRENT BANK BALANCE
JLA102477	128	10
MA 102176	235	25
KB 163065	100	50
PB 147672	131	8
CAB135945	150	30
CHB135916	243	20
JB 149853	129	10
LEB165394	137	4
SCB163066	110	5

Figure 38. A daily banking printout on each client gives total tokens earned for the years as well as the current balance.

CARD FORMAT

JOB-TOKEN-PERCENTAGE DECK

Col 1-3 Initials	Col 5-10 Client Number	Col 11-16 Date	Col 17-80 Jobs-Tokens-Percentages
			17-19 Job Number
			20-21 Tokens Earned
		11-12 Mo.	22-24 Percentage
		13-14 Day	25-27 Job Number
		15-16 Yr.	28-29 Tokens Earned
			30-32 Percentage
			Etc.

Figure 39. The card format for recording the type of job, tokens earned, and percentage earned on each job description over any number of days.

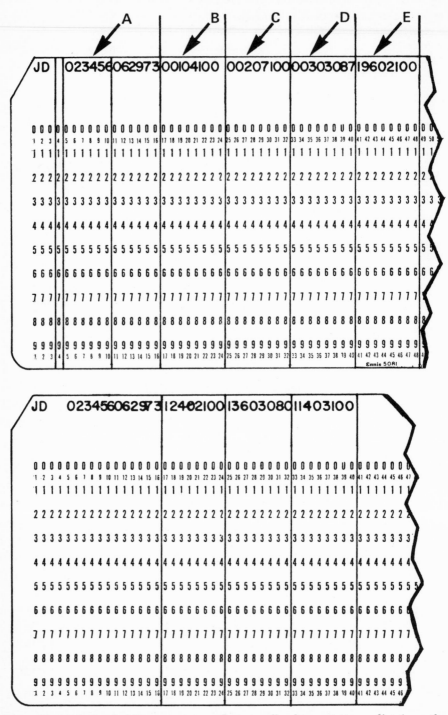

Figure 40. Analysis of this computer card can easily demonstrate a client's work activities, tokens earned, and percentages obtained for the day without having to handle excessive amounts of paper.

PROGRAM SETUP FOR COMPUTER GRAPHS

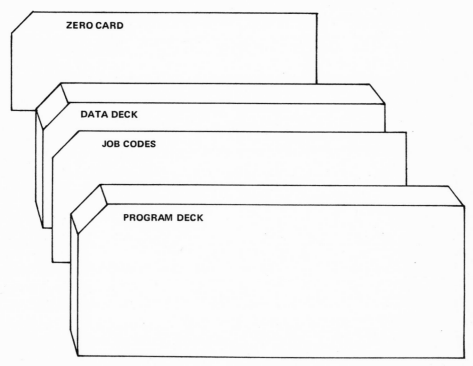

Figure 41. The program setup for the production of computer plots which can be graphed to depict client performance.

tokens, keypunched 03 and functioned at a level of 30 percent, keypunched 030. Code 014 shows his resource room assignment of watching a filmstrip and earning three tokens, keypunched 03 and functioning at a level of 80 percent, keypunched 080, on his criterion test. Code 016 reflects his phonics assignment earning him two tokens and functioning at a level of 50 percent. His work job descriptions begin a second card in column seventeen. Code 124 shows he dust mopped for which he earned two tokens and functioned at a level of 100 percent. His 136 code is hand dusting and he earned three tokens at a level of 80 percent. Code 114 is hand sanding for which he earned three tokens and functioned at a level of 100 percent.

Cards as shown in Figure 40 are accumulated for clients over an eight- to ten-week period. They are put into a program setup as shown in Figure 41 and graphs are plotted as shown in Figure 42.

The graphs shown in Figure 42 may have one, two or three job descriptions plotted on one printout. This graphic representation is the performance level attained by client JD 023456 for the job description code 002, punctuality. The graph is on a scale of 0 to 100 percent and depicts the

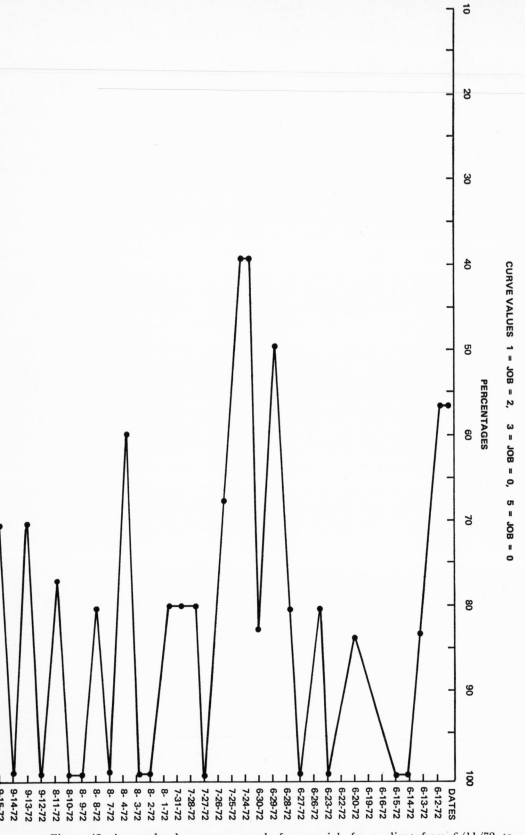

Figure 42. A completed computer graph for one job for a client from 6/11/72 to 9/15/72.

client's daily performance from 6/12/72 to 9/15/72. The graph plots an average performance of approximately 80 percent for this period of time.

ANALYSIS OF CLIENT PERFORMANCE

The data that are reported in this chapter may easily reflect a client's spending patterns. An almost effortless analysis can be made to determine the items for which the client is spending his earned tokens. A determination can be made, from observation of his banking, whether he is saving, utilizing the checking system and for what items he is working. The same analysis can be made on all clients to determine overall spending patterns for the economy. Spending pattern information may help regulate the inflation and/or deflation of pricing reinforcing contingencies.

The economic structure, in order to attain the maximum performance efficiency on the part of the client, should require only a minimal banking balance for each client. A client with a large banking balance is likely to have low performance rates as compared to a client with a low balance unless saving is a highly positively reinforcing contingency.

Diagnostically, these data are invaluable for the daily maintenance of the system. An extremely important and necessary usage of the data is the reflection of improved client performance as a result of the treatment procedure.

CHAPTER 9

RESEARCH

T HE RECOMMENDATIONS MADE in this book are based on an exemplary program at the Center for Developmental and Learning Disorders (CDLD), a university affiliated facility, which is part of the University of Alabama in Birmingham. The program outlined in prior chapters is a research and training project and is part of the total CDLD program.

DATA

The data collected on this project was for the express purpose of identifying an appropriate program for the Division of Special Education and Vocational Rehabilitation of the CDLD to recommend as a tried and true procedure for other similar programs. The program has proven effective over a three-year period, and its application is varied to more facilities and agencies than were originally considered.

The data reported here involves the original baseline information on twenty-two educable mentally retarded vocational rehabilitation clients. The data involves a thirteen-day period without extrinsically reinforcing contingencies and a ten-day period of treatment.

Replication over behaviors and over subjects' design was utilized due not only to the practicality and necessity for applied research, but for the fact that replication is a strong proof. The use of this procedure was considered as strong a proof as a reversal procedure and did not require termination of treatment.

Three behaviors for each of the twenty-two subjects are presented in Figures 43 through 64 to demonstrate the effectiveness of the open token economy system. A twelve-day period from November 4, 1970, to November 20, 1970, was the initial baseline period. A two-week period from November 23, 1970, until December 4, 1970, was the initial treatment period. These data demonstrate a significant performance change in nearly all of the clients used as subjects in the program.

Further proof of the program effectiveness is the lack of resistance or non-responsiveness by subjects to the treatment process. Ayllon and Azrin (1968) reported 18 percent of their chronic schizophrenic patients were unresponsive to the reinforcement. Zimmerman, Zimmerman and Russell (1969) reported that three of seven retardates were unaffected by token

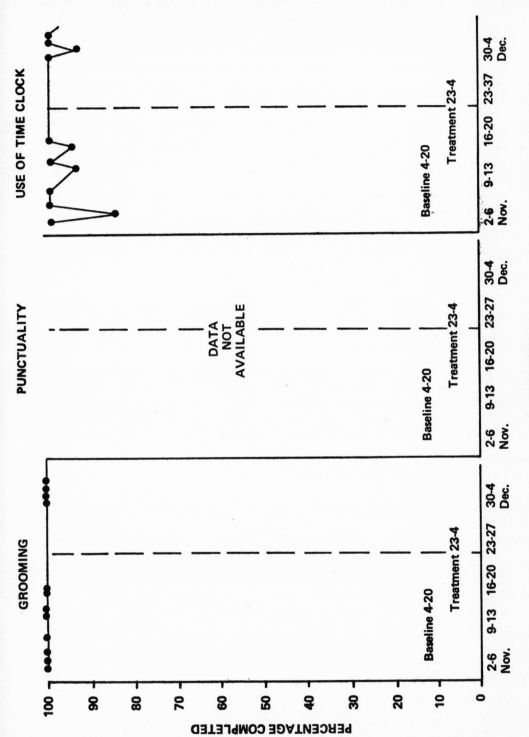

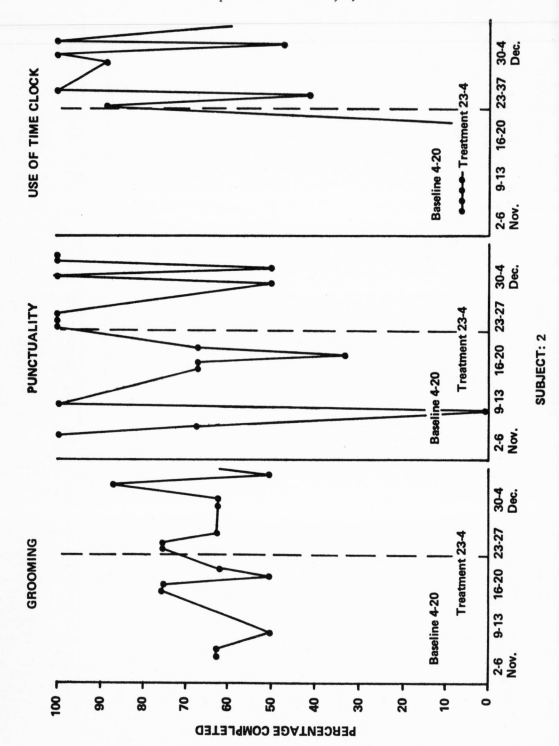

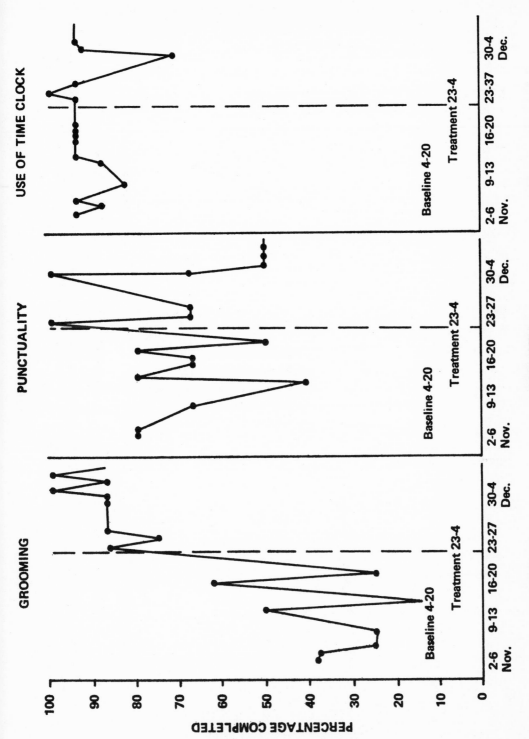

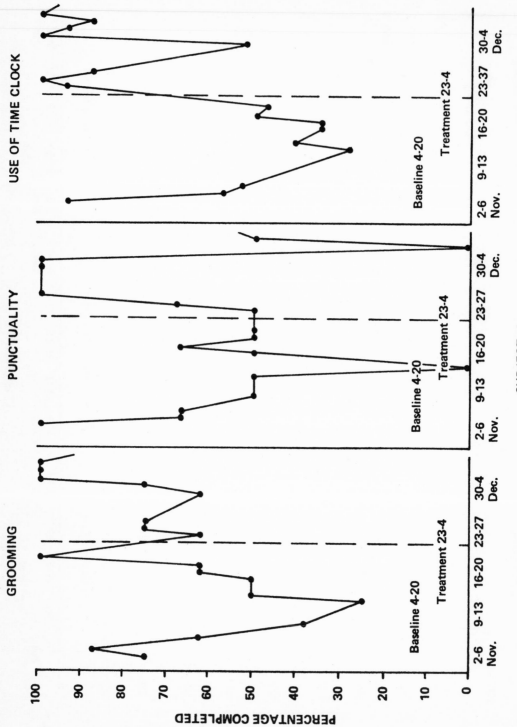

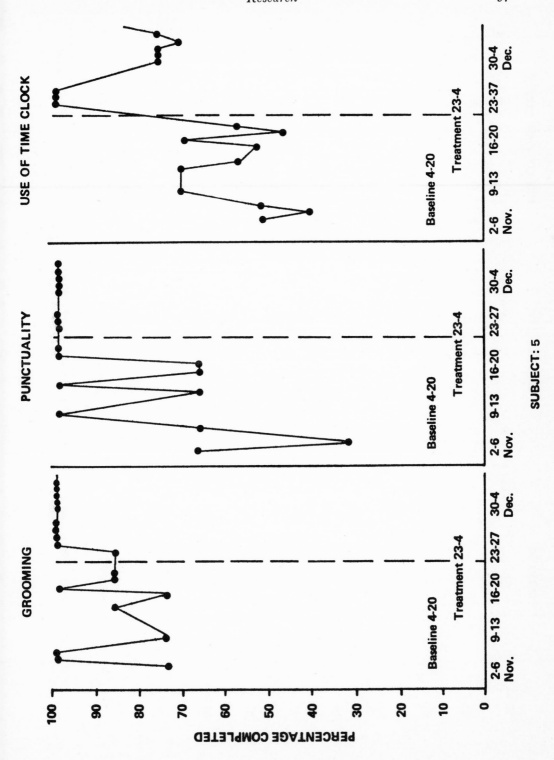

USE OF TIME CLOCK

PUNCTUALITY

GROOMING

PERCENTAGE COMPLETED

SUBJECT: 5

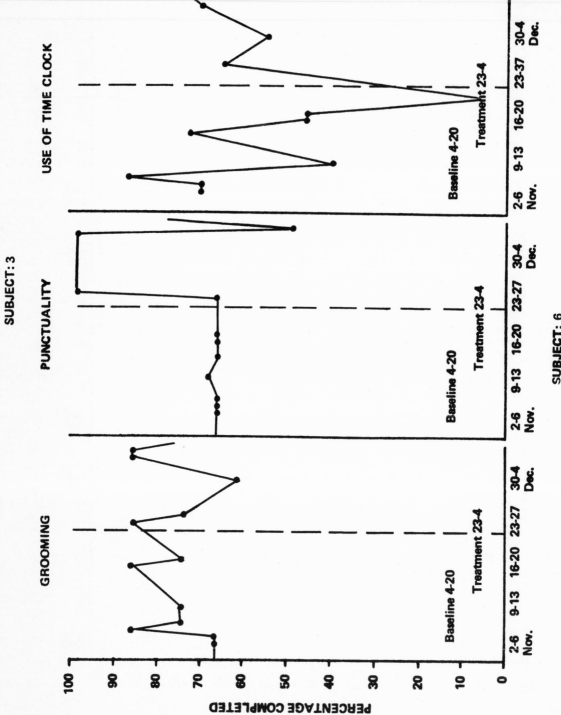

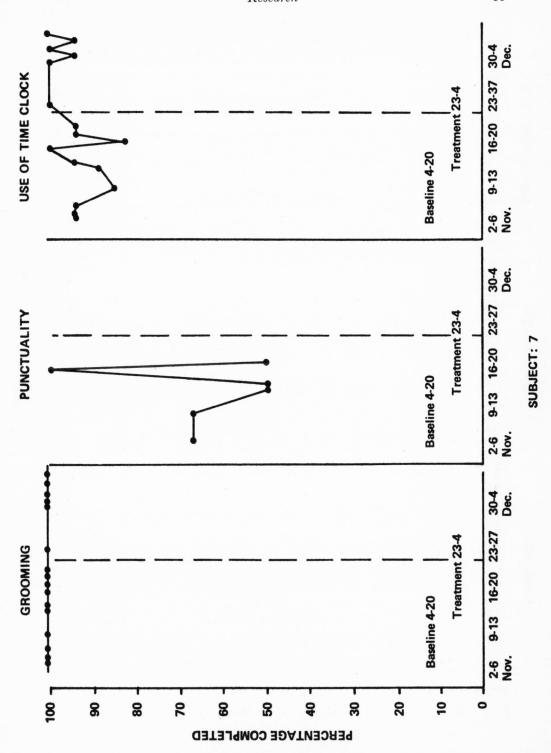

SUBJECT: 7

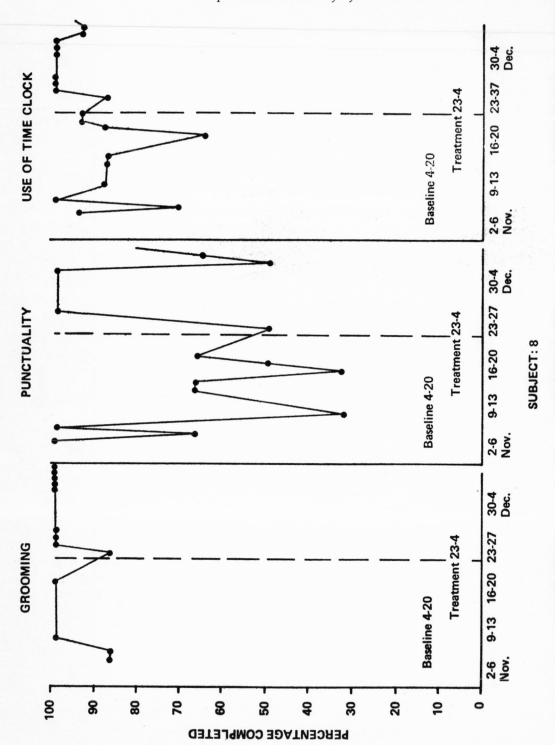

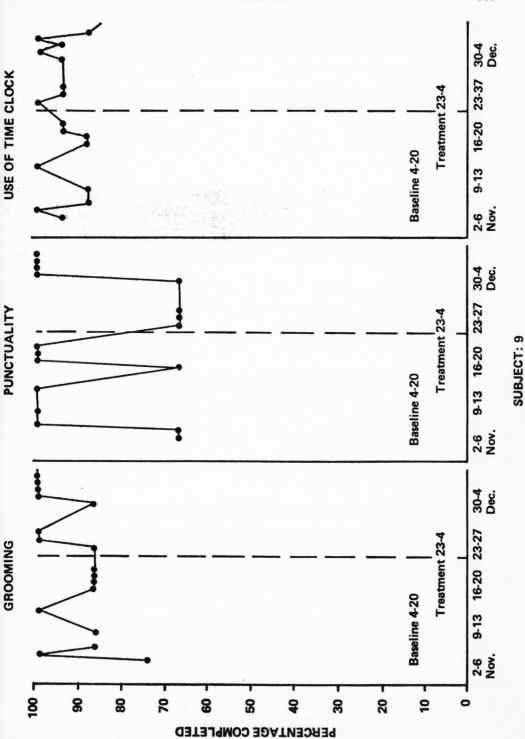

SUBJECT: 9

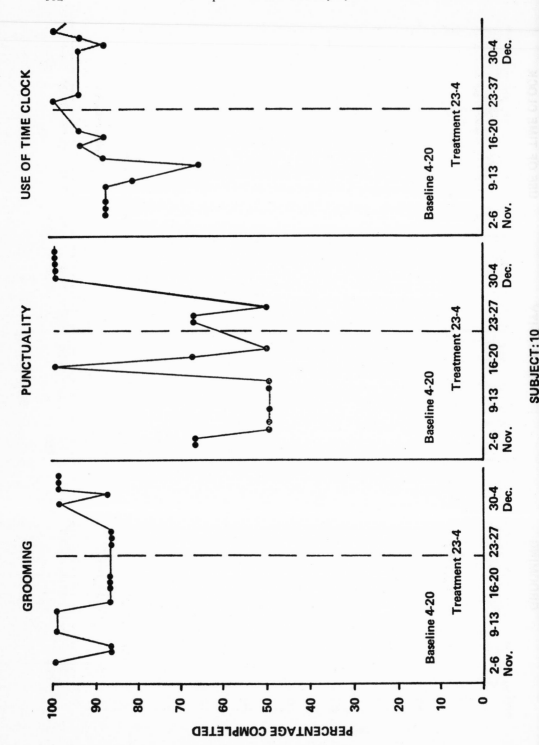

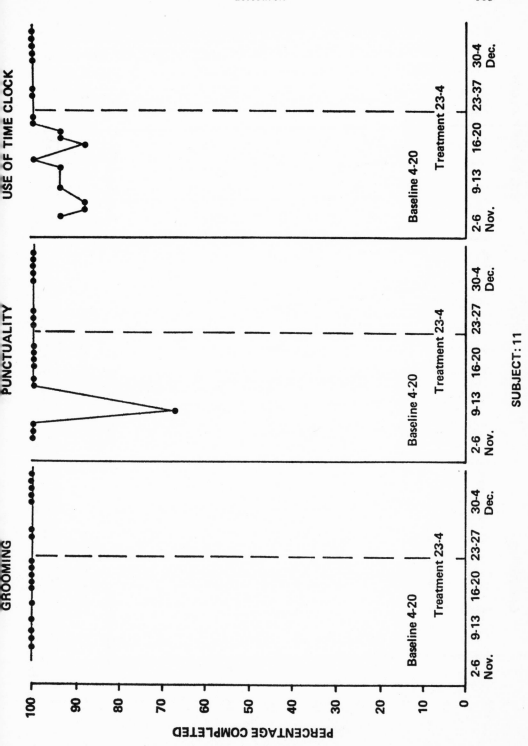

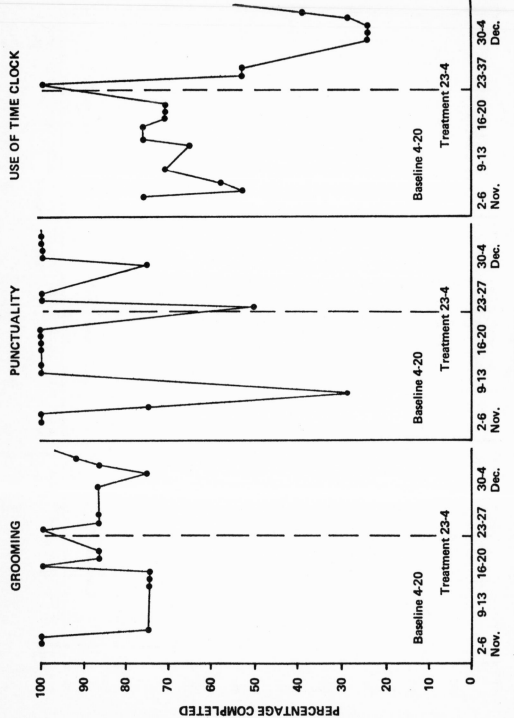

SUBJECT: 12

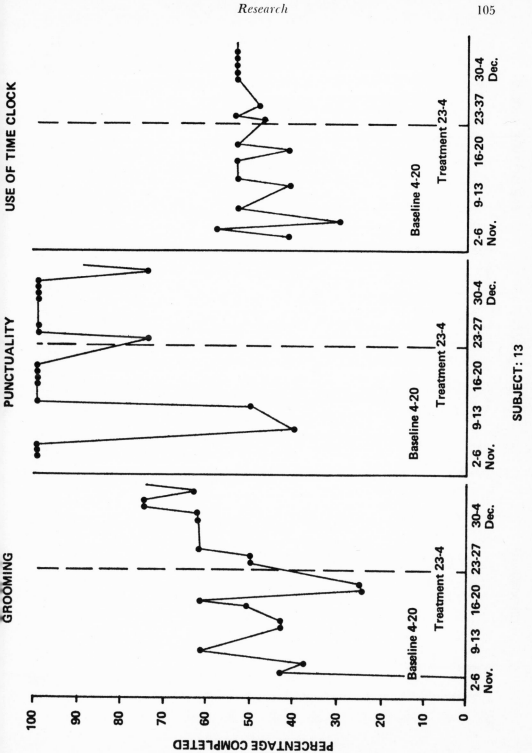

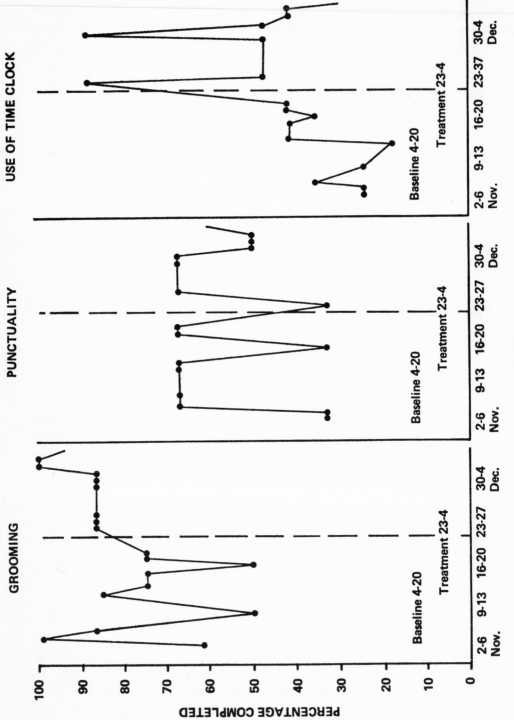

SUBJECT: 14

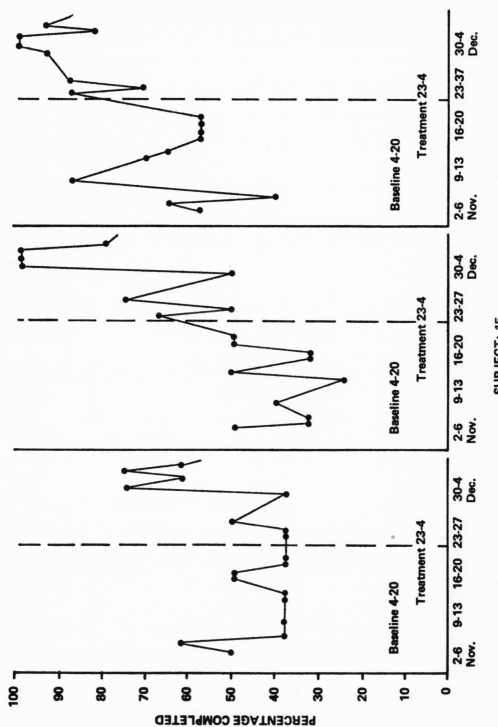

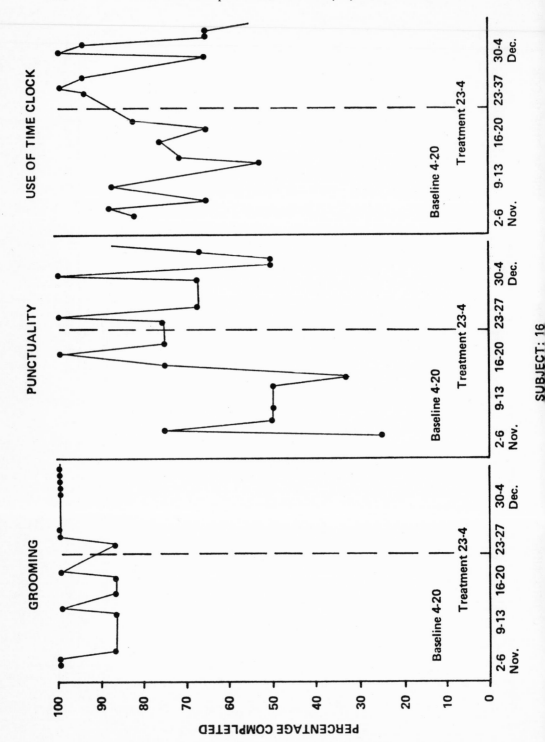

SUBJECT: 16

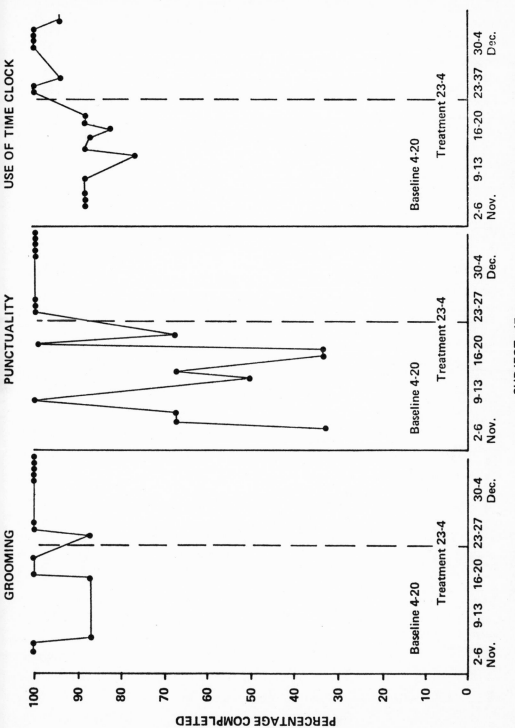

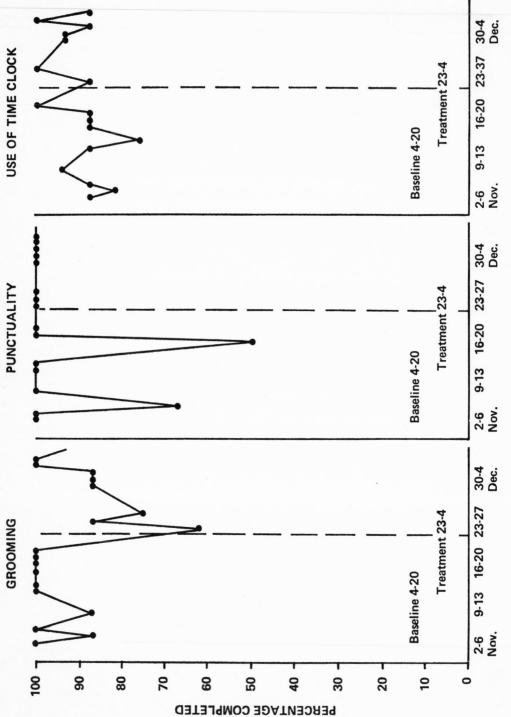

SUBJECT: 18

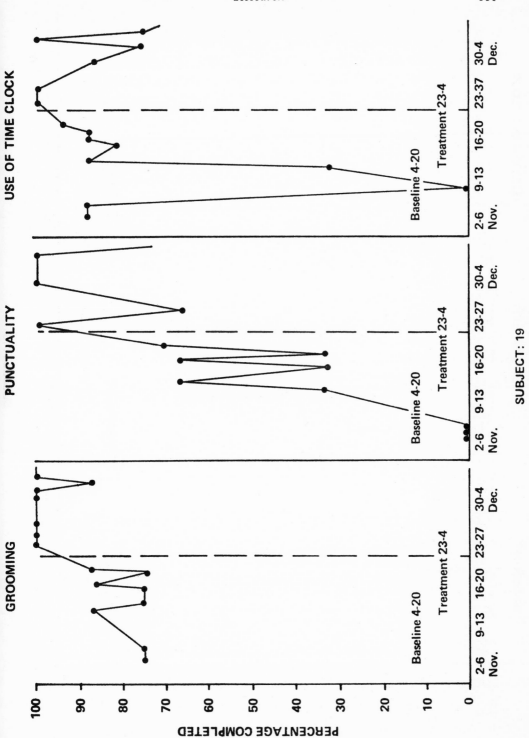

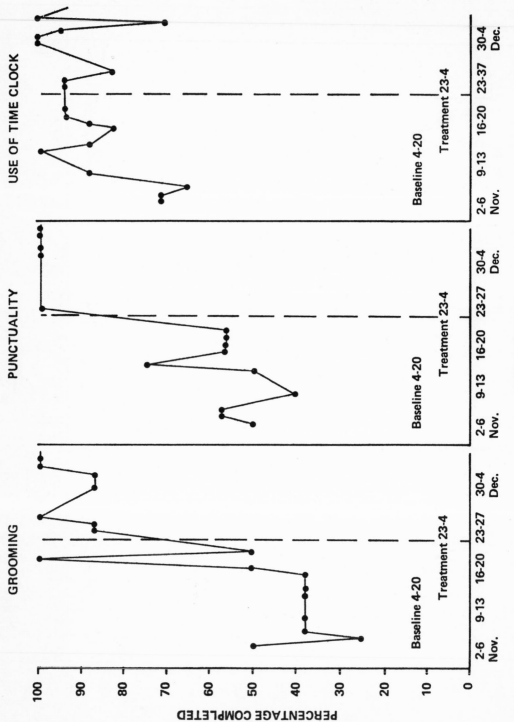

SUBJECT: 20

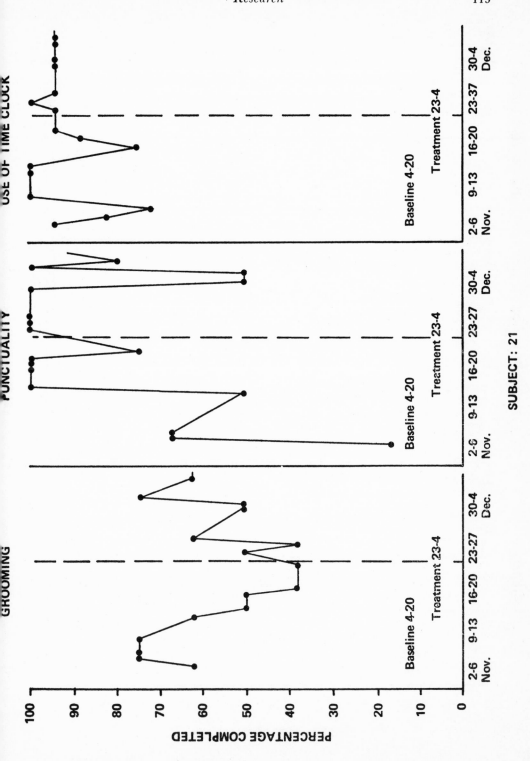

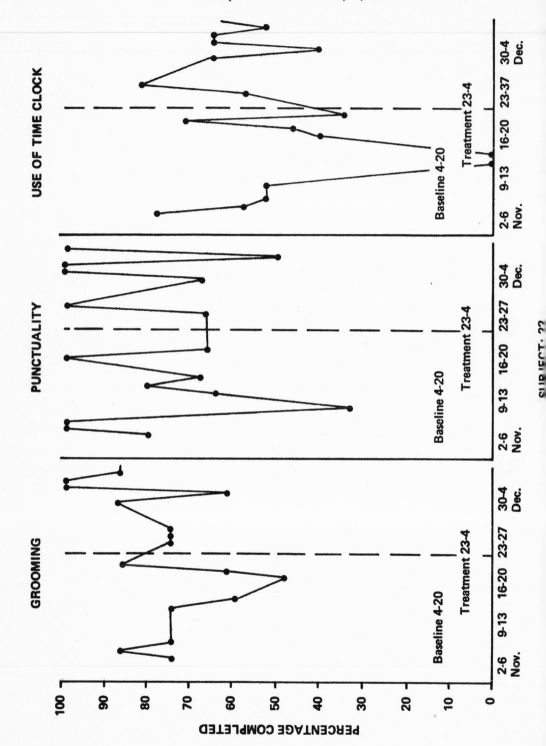

SUBJECT: 22

reinforcement. Ray and Sheldon (1968) similarly indicate a 13 percent unresponsive rate with disturbed adolescent retardates.

The majority of the economies reported (Atthowe, 1967; Ayllon and Azrin, 1968; Chase, 1970; Girardeau and Spradlin, 1964; Lent, 1967; Phillips, 1968; Ross, 1967; Tyler and Brown, 1968) are closed systems; that is, the subjects are under twenty-four hour control. The program reported here is for day treatment.

The data reported here demonstrates that 14 percent of the graphs (nine of sixty-six reported) showed no significant improvement over the baseline period, and 9 percent of the subjects (two out of twenty-two) demonstrated no significant improvement over baseline on three reported behaviors.

The daily and weekly reporting of the data is for program justification; however, these data are of more benefit as a diagnostic instrument for identification of inadequately performed job related behaviors. These behaviors can be given attention for each client individually.

The program's purpose is not program proof but job placement and employment stability. Present statistics on the initial twenty-two clients reflect that 37 percent are employed full time, 50 percent are employed at part time or full time jobs and 22 percent of the clients are still enrolled in the program. Eighteen percent of the clients were referred to other rehabilitation programs. The remaining 10 percent (two out of twenty-two subjects) are neither enrolled in a rehabilitation program nor employed.

The average age of these original clients was approximately seventeen years in 1970. The data have reflected that only two of the twenty-two clients are total failures within a three-year period. It should also be noted here that none of the subjects were terminated as a function of maladaptive behavior or absenteeism. The two failures are a function of a degenerative brain syndrome in one case and physical inability to perform the work (hemiplegia) in the other case.

PROPOSED RESEARCH

Research possibilities for the open token economy are numerous. The job description can be administered to numerous subjects who have been assigned to jobs to ascertain predictive validity of the descriptions; the job description may be checked by numerous observers to ascertain the reliability of the measuring device as well as its objectivity; comparisons of success criterion of job descriptions with success or failure on the job; application of the procedures of the economy to another population of handicapped individuals; comparative studies of similar programs which do not utilize the procedures outlined in this book.

The ultimate project would be a design which pitted the token economy procedure with a matched group of individuals which went through a traditional rehabilitation program.

The data, on some of the clients, were observed to be at a high percentage on baseline and required little change. These data are only sample behaviors and were chosen because these are the only behaviors which remain the same across subjects on a daily basis. Even with a high rate of responding on baseline, improvement was noted after treatment was instituted. This observation raises the research question as to which group or level of handicapping conditions would profit most from the open token economy system.

REFERENCES

Ayllon, T., and Azrin, N.: *The Token Economy: A Motivational System for Therapy and Rehabilitation.* New York, Appleton, 1968.

Atthowe, J. M.: *Ward 203C, Token Program: Manual for Ward Staff.* Unpublished manuscript, Veterans Administration Hospital, Palo Alto, California, 1967.

Baker, R. J., and Sawyer, H. W.: *Adjustment Services in Rehabilitation: Emphasis on Human Change.* Auburn, Auburn University, 1971.

Bensberg, G. J., and Barnett, C. D.: *Attendant Training in Southern Residential Facilities for the Mentally Retarded: Report of the SREB Attendant Training Project.* Atlanta, Southern Regional Education Board, 1966.

Bensberg, G. J.: *Teaching the Mentally Retarded: A Handbook for Ward Personnel.* Atlanta, Southern Regional Education Board, 1965.

Birnbrauer, J. S., Bijou, S. W., Wolf, M. M., and Kidder, J. D.: Programmed instruction in the classroom. In Ullmann, L. P., and Krasner, L. (Eds.) : *Case Studies in Behavior Modification.* New York, HR&W, 1965.

Birnbrauer, J. S., Wolf, M. M., Kidder, J. D., and Taque, C. E.: Classroom behavior of retarded pupils with token reinforcement. In Sloane, H. N., and Macaulay, B. D. (Eds.) : *Operant Procedures in Remedial Speech and Language Training.* Boston, HM, 1968.

Bloom, B. S.: *Taxonomy of Educational Objectives: The Classification of Educational Goals, Handbook I: Cognitive Domain.* New York, McKay, 1956.

Boren, J. J., and Colman, A. D.: Some experiments on reinforcement principles within a psychiatric ward for delinquent soldiers. *J Appl Behav Anal, 3:29,* 1970.

Buckley, Nancy K., and Walker, H. M.: *Modifying Classroom Behavior: A Manual of Procedure for Classroom Teachers.* Champaign, Res Press, 1970.

Cantrell, R. P., Cantrell, Mary L., Huddleston, C. M., and Wooldridge, R. L.: Contingency contracting with school problems. *J Appl Behav Anal, 2:215,* 1969.

Chase, J. D.: Token economy programs in the Veterans Administration. V.A. Department of Medicine and Surgery, Washington, D.C., 1970.

Dalton, A. J., Rubino, C. A., and Hislop, M. W.: Some effects of token rewards on school achievement of children with Down's Syndrome. *J Appl Behav Anal, 6:251,* 1973.

Dunn, D. S.: *Situational Assessment: Model for the Future.* Menomonie, University of Wisconsin-Stout, 1973.

Fisher, R. A.: *Statistical Methods for Research Workers,* 10th ed. Edinburgh, Oliver and Boyd, Ltd., 1948.

Girardeau, F. L., and Spradlin, J. E.: Token rewards in a cottage program. *Ment Retard, 2:345,* 1964.

Gist, J. W., and Welch, M. W.: *The Open Token Economy: A Training Manual.* Birmingham, Center for Developmental and Learning Disorders, 1972.

Heber, R. F.: *A Manual on Terminology and Classification in Mental Retardation.* Am J Ment Defic, 1959.

Homme, L.: Human motivation and the environment. In Haring, N., and Whelan, R. (Eds.) : *The Learning Environment: Relationship to Behavior Modification and Implications for Special Education.* Lawrence, U Pr of Kansas, 1966.

Homme, L., Csanyi, A., Gonzales, M., and Rachs, J.: *How to Use Contingency Contracting in the Classroom.* Champaign, Res Press, 1969.

House, Betty J., and Zeaman, D.: A comparison of discrimination learning in normal and mentally defective children. *Child Dev, 29:411,* 1958 (a).

House, Betty J., and Zeaman, D.: Visual discrimination learning in imbeciles. *Am J Ment Defic, 63:447,* 1958 (b).

Ingham, R. J., and Andrews, G.: An analysis of token economy in stuttering therapy. *J Appl Behav Anal, 6:219,* 1973.

Kazdin, A. E., and Bootzin, R. R.: The token economy: An evaluative review. *J Appl Behav Anal, 5:343,* 1972.

Kirk, S. A.: *Educating Exceptional Children,* 2nd Ed. Boston, HM, 1972.

Kolstoe, O. P.: *Teaching Educable Mentally Retarded Children.* New York, HR&W, 1970.

Kvaraceus, W. C., and Miller, W. B.: *Delinquent Behavior: Culture and the Individual.* Washington, NEA, 1959.

Lent, J. R.: A demonstration program for intensive training of institutionalized mentally retarded girls. Progress Report, U.S. Department of Health, Education, and Welfare, January, 1967.

Logan, D. L.: A paper money token system as a recording aid in institutional settings. *J Appl Behav Anal, 3:183,* 1970.

Mager, R. F.: *Preparing Instructional Objectives.* Belmont, Fearon, 1962.

Newland, T. E.: Psychological assessment of exceptional children and youth. In Cruickshank, W. M. (Ed.) : *Psychology of Exceptional Children and Youth.* Englewood Cliffs, P-H, 1963.

Patterson, G. R., and Guillion, M.: *Living with Children: New Methods for Parents and Teachers.* Champaign, Res Press, 1968.

Phillips, E. L., Phillips, Elaine A., Fixsen, D. L., and Wolf, M. M.: Achievement place: Modification of the behavior of predelinquent boys within a token economy. *J Appl Behav Anal, 1:213,* 1968.

Ray, E. T., and Shelton, J. T.: The use of operant conditioning with adolescent retarded boys. Paper presented at the 20th Mental Hospital Institute, Washington, D.C., October, 1968.

Robinson, H. B., and Robinson, Nancy M.: *The Mentally Retarded Child: A Psychological Approach.* New York, McGraw, 1965.

Ross, R. R.: Application of operant conditioning procedures to the behavior of institutionalized adolescent offenders. University of Waterloo, Unpublished Manuscript, 1967.

Sankovsky, R.: *State of the Art in Vocational Evaluation: Report of a National Survey.* Pittsburgh, University of Pittsburgh, 1969.

Santogross, D. A., O'Leary, D. K., Romanczyk, R. G., and Kaufman, K. F.: Self-evaluation by adolescents in a psychiatric hospital school token program. *J Appl Behav Anal, 6:277,* 1973.

Saylor, J. G., and Alexander, W. M.: *Curriculum Planning for Modern Schools.* New York, HR&W, 1966.

Schaefer, H. H., and Martin, P. L.: *Behavioral Therapy.* New York, McGraw, 1969.

Szasz, T. S.: The myth of mental illness. *American Psychologist, 15:*113, 1960.

Szasz, T. S.: The uses of naming and the origin of the myth of mental illness. *Am Psychol, 16:*59, 1961 (a) .

Taber, J. L., Glaser, R., and Schaefer, H. H.: *Learning and Programmed Instruction.* Reading, A-W, 1965.

Thomson, W. R.: Early environment: Its importance for later behavior. In Hoch, P., and Zubin, Z. (Eds.) : *Psychopathology of Childhood.* New York, Grune, 1955.

Tyler, V. O., and Brown, G. D.: Token reinforcement of academic performance with institutionalized delinquent boys. *J Educ Psychol, 59:*164, 1968.

Welch, M. W., and Carpenter, C.: Solution of a school phobia by contingency contracting. *School Application of Learning Theory.* Kalamazoo, Kalamazoo Intermediate School District, 2 (3) , 1970.

Zimmerman, E. H., and Zimmerman, J.: The alteration of behavior in a special class situation. In Ullmann, L. P., and Krasner, L. (Eds.) : *Case Studies in Behavior Modification.* New York, HR&W, 1965.

Zimmerman, E. H., Zimmerman, J., and Russell, C. D.: Differential effects of token reinforcement on instruction-following behavior in retarded students instructed as a group. *J Appl Behav Anal, 2:*101, 1969.

APPENDICES

APPENDIX A

EXAMPLES OF
BLUE LEVEL JOB DESCRIPTIONS

CENTER FOR DEVELOPMENTAL AND LEARNING DISORDERS

TOKEN ECONOMY

1/19/72   NAME_____

DATE_____

TRACING LEATHER PATTERN
TOKEN VALUE 3

YES   NO

_____ 1. OBTAIN TOOLS TO BE USED: A. SCISSORS; B. PENCIL; C. PATTERN;
            D. LEATHER PUNCH; E. CARDBOARD SHEET

_____ 2. TRACE AROUND THE PATTERN WITH PENCIL ONTO THE CARD-
            BOARD SHEET.

_____ 3. MAKE SURE TRACED PATTERN HAS NO DIFFERENCES FROM
            ORIGINAL PATTERN.

_____ 4. CUT OUT PATTERN WITH SCISSORS.

_____ 5. MAKE SURE THAT CUT PATTERN HAS NO DIFFERENCES FROM THE
            ORIGINAL PATTERN.

_____ 6. PUNCH DESIGNATED HOLES INTO PATTERN WITH LEATHER
            PUNCH.

_____ 7. CLEAN WORK AREA.

_____ 8. INFORM SUPERVISOR WHEN COMPLETED.

TIME FINISHED _____

TIME STARTED _____

TOTAL TIME _____

CODE 119

TOKENS _____

PERCENTAGE _____ %

121

CENTER FOR DEVELOPMENTAL AND LEARNING DISORDERS
TOKEN ECONOMY

10/22/71   NAME_____

                                      DATE_____

CLEANING BATHROOM LAVATORY

TOKEN VALUE 2

YES   NO

_____ 1. ASSEMBLE SUPPLIES ON TRAY:
                A. CLOTHS   B. CLEANSER

_____ 2. SPRINKLE CLEANSER ON DAMP CLOTH AND SCRUB ALL SURFACES
                OF THE SINK, RINSING CLOTH AND RESPRINKLING CLOTH WITH
                CLEANSER AS OFTEN AS NEEDED.

_____ 3. RINSE RAG AND SQUEEZE IT UNTIL IT IS ONLY MOIST—WIPE SOAP
                FROM ALL SURFACES CLEANED.

_____ 4. SCRUB AND RINSE SOAP DISH.

_____ 5. WIPE OFF CORD, SPRAY HEAD, AND SPRAY HOLDER.

_____ 6. POLISH ALL CHROME SURFACES WITH A DRY CLOTH.

_____ 7. DRY SOAP AND REPLACE IT IN SOAP DISH. RUB AND POLISH SINK
                SURFACE UNTIL NO STREAKS ARE VISIBLE.

_____ 8. CLEAN SUPPLIES AND PUT THEM AWAY.

_____ 9. MOP UP ANY WATER THAT YOU SPILL.

_____ 10. INFORM SUPERVISOR WHEN FINISHED.

WORKS AT STEADY PACE:

EXCESSIVE TALKING - NO. TIMES _____   TIME FINISHED _____

LEAVING WORK AREA - NO. TIMES _____   TIME STARTED _____

IDLE - NUMBER TIMES _____   TOTAL TIME _____

CODE   021

TOKENS _____

PERCENTAGE _____%

**CENTER FOR DEVELOPMENTAL AND LEARNING DISORDERS
TOKEN ECONOMY**

10/13/72

NAME_____

DATE_____

HAND SAWING

TOKEN VALUE 3 per ½ hour

YES   NO

_____ 1. SELECT PROPER SAW FOR JOB TO BE DONE (CARPENTER, COPING, KEYHOLE, HACKSAW).

_____ 2. MAKE FIRST FIVE CUTS WITH SHORT STROKES.

_____ 3. CONTINUE CUTTING WITH LONG FIRM STROKES.

_____ 4. HOLD OBJECT TO BE CUT WITH HAND, VISE, OR HAVE SOMEONE HOLD IT FOR YOU.

_____ 5. MAKE CERTAIN THAT FINISHING STROKES ARE SHORT AND OBJECT BEING CUT IS HELD FIRMLY TO PREVENT TEARING.

_____ 6. RETURN SAW AND UNUSED WOOD TO PROPER PLACE.

_____ 7. CLEAN WORK AREA.

_____ 8. INFORM SUPERVISOR WHEN JOB IS FINISHED.

WORKS AT STEADY PACE:

EXCESSIVE TALKING - NO. TIMES_____   TIME FINISHED_____

LEAVING WORK AREA - NO. TIMES_____   TIME STARTED_____

IDLE - NUMBER TIMES_____   TOTAL TIME_____

CODE 082

TOKENS_____

PERCENTAGE_____%

CENTER FOR DEVELOPMENTAL AND LEARNING DISORDERS
TOKEN ECONOMY

11/15/72

NAME_____

DATE_____

SPIRIT PROCESS DUPLICATOR

TOKEN VALUE 3 per ½ hour

YES   NO

_____ 1. REMOVE PROTECTIVE COVER FROM MACHINE.

_____ 2. TURN SPIRIT CONTAINER UPSIDE DOWN TO FILL WELL WITH LIQUID.

_____ 3. MOVE LIQUID REGULATOR TO CENTER OF BAR.

_____ 4. MOVE PRESSURE LEVEL TO YOUR RIGHT AS FAR AS IT WILL GO.

_____ 5. TEAR OFF AND PLACE SPIRIT MASTER UPSIDE DOWN ON CYLINDER AND CLOSE LOCK.

_____ 6. PLACE SCRAP PAPER IN PAPER TRAY AND RUN TRIAL COPIES.

_____ 7. REMOVE SCRAP PAPER AND REPLACE WITH MIMEOGRAPH PAPER.

_____ 8. RUN REQUESTED NUMBER OF COPIES.

_____ 9. REMOVE SPIRIT MASTER FROM CYLINDER AND PLACE WITH PRINTED COPIES.

_____ 10. IF NO MORE SPIRIT MASTERS ARE TO BE RUN:
    A. MOVE PRESSURE LEVEL TO LEFT AS FAR AS IT WILL GO.
    B. MOVE LIQUID REGULATOR TOWARD YOURSELF.
    C. TURN LIQUID CONTAINER WITH SPOUT UP.

_____ 11. PUT PROTECTIVE COVER ON MACHINE.

_____ 12. DELIVER COPIES TO DESIGNATED ROOMS ON REQUEST FORM AND RETURN IMMEDIATELY.

_____ 13. INFORM SUPERVISOR WHEN JOB IS FINISHED.

WORKS AT STEADY PACE:

EXCESSIVE TALKING - NO. TIMES _____   TIME FINISHED _____

LEAVING WORK AREA - NO. TIMES _____   TIME STARTED _____

IDLE - NUMBER TIMES _____   TOTAL TIME _____

CODE 104

TOKENS _____

PERCENTAGE _____ %

CENTER FOR DEVELOPMENTAL AND LEARNING DISORDERS
TOKEN ECONOMY

10/22/71   NAME_____

                                         DATE_____

WET MOPPING

TOKEN VALUE 4

YES   NO

_____   1. ASSEMBLE SUPPLIES AND EQUIPMENT:
                   MOP   BUCKET
                   SOAP   CLOTHS

_____   2. FILL BUCKET HALF FULL OF WARM WATER.

_____   3. PUT THE CORRECT MEASURE OF CLEANER INTO BUCKET.

_____   4. DAMPEN MOP.

_____   5. SQUEEZE MOP OUT DRY.

_____   6. GO OVER AREA TO BE CLEANED IN SMALL SECTIONS UNTIL AREA
                   HAS BEEN COMPLETELY MOPPED. MOP WALKING BACKWARD SO
                   AS NOT TO TRACK OVER MOPPED AREA.

_____   7. RINSE MOP AND BUCKET.

_____   8. FILL BUCKET HALF FULL OF COOL WATER.

_____   9. DAMPEN MOP IN RINSE WATER AND WRING MOP DRY.

_____   10. GO OVER FLOOR RINSING SMALL SECTIONS AT A TIME UNTIL
                   AREA HAS BEEN COMPLETELY RINSED.

_____   11. RINSE MOP AND GO OVER MOPPED AREA THOROUGHLY TO TAKE
                   UP ANY EXCESS WATER. RINSE OUT BUCKET AND MOP.

_____   12. DRY OUT BUCKET. PUT AWAY SUPPLIES AND EQUIPMENT
                   PROPERLY.

_____   13. INFORM SUPERVISOR WHEN FINISHED.

WORKS AT STEADY PACE:

EXCESSIVE TALKING - NO. TIMES _____   TIME FINISHED _____

LEAVING WORK AREA - NO. TIMES _____   TIME STARTED _____

IDLE - NUMBER TIMES _____   TOTAL TIME _____

CODE   135

TOKENS _____

PERCENTAGE _____ %

CENTER FOR DEVELOPMENTAL AND LEARNING DISORDERS
TOKEN ECONOMY

2/15/72   NAME_____

AREA_____   DATE_____

SWEEPING

TOKEN VALUE 2

YES   NO

_____   1. ASSEMBLE SUPPLIES AND EQUIPMENT:
                    BROOM, DUSTPAN, TRASH CAN

_____   2. SWEEP AREA WITH SHORT MOVEMENTS OF THE BROOM.

_____   3. WORK FROM THE CORNER OF A ROOM PULLING SWEEPINGS FROM
                    UNDER FURNITURE AND APPLIANCES.

_____   4. BRUSH ALL SWEEPINGS INTO DUSTPAN.

_____   5. EMPTY DUSTPAN INTO TRASH CAN.

_____   6. DUST OFF SWEEPING EDGE OF BROOM INTO TRASH CAN.

_____   7. EMPTY TRASH CAN.

_____   8. PLACE TRASH CAN IN PROPER PLACE. PUT AWAY BROOM AND
                    DUSTPAN.

_____   9. INFORM SUPERVISOR WHEN TASK IS COMPLETED.

                                    TIME FINISHED _____

                                    TIME STARTED _____

                                    TOTAL TIME _____

                                    CODE 034

                                    TOKENS _____

                                    PERCENTAGE _____ %

CENTER FOR DEVELOPMENTAL AND LEARNING DISORDERS
TOKEN ECONOMY

4/3/72

NAME_____

DATE_____

STAINING

TOKEN VALUE 3 per ½ hour

YES   NO

_____ 1. SELECT PROPER STAIN.

_____ 2. SELECT CLEAN RAGS OR BRUSH.

_____ 3. SELECT AND INSPECT WOOD FOR NICKS, CUTS, AND SCRATCHES.

_____ 4. START STAINING WITH SHORT STROKES FOLLOWING WOOD GRAIN.

_____ 5. APPLY STAIN EVENLY TO SURFACE.

_____ 6. DISCARD RAGS OR CLEAN UP BRUSHES.

_____ 7. CLEAN WORK AREA.

_____ 8. REPLACE TOOLS.

_____ 9. INFORM SUPERVISOR WHEN JOB IS COMPLETED.

WORKS AT STEADY PACE:

EXCESSIVE TALKING - NO. TIMES _____   TIME FINISHED _____

LEAVING WORK AREA - NO. TIMES _____   TIME STARTED _____

IDLE - NUMBER TIMES _____   TOTAL TIME _____

CODE 151

TOKENS _____

PERCENTAGE _____%

CENTER FOR DEVELOPMENTAL AND LEARNING DISORDERS
TOKEN ECONOMY

1/6/72

NAME_____

DATE_____

LACING KEY CASE

TOKEN VALUE 3 per ½ hour

YES   NO   *NOTE: FILL IN STITCH TO BE USED
                                      BEFORE STUDENT-CLIENT BEGINS
_____ 1. GET PROPER KIT.   WORKING ON JOB DESCRIPTION.

_____ 2. GET LACING NEEDLE.

_____ 3. PLACE LACING LEATHER INTO NEEDLE.

_____ 4. PLACE PIECES TO BE ASSEMBLED OVER EACH OTHER IN PROPER
                ALIGNMENT.

_____ 5. BEGIN TO LACE AT THE RIGHT PLACE.

_____ 6. LACE PROJECT USING _____* STITCH.

_____ 7. DO NOT TWIST LACING.

_____ 8. WHEN FINISHED RETURN ALL TOOLS TO PROPER PLACE.

_____ 9. CLEAN UP WORK AREA.

_____ 10. INFORM SUPERVISOR WHEN JOB IS FINISHED.

WORKS AT STEADY PACE:

   EXCESSIVE TALKING - NO. TIMES_____   TIME FINISHED _____

   LEAVING WORK AREA - NO. TIMES_____   TIME STARTED _____

   IDLE - NUMBER TIMES _____   TOTAL TIME _____

   CODE 090

   TOKENS _____

   PERCENTAGE _____%

CENTER FOR DEVELOPMENTAL AND LEARNING DISORDERS
TOKEN ECONOMY

10/22/71   NAME_____

AREA_____   DATE_____

CLEANING GREEN CHALK BOARDS & ERASERS

TOKEN VALUE 3

YES   NO
_____ 1. ASSEMBLE SUPPLIES:
                   A. THREE CLEAN, DRY CLOTHS   C. PORTABLE VACUUM CLEANER
                   B. DIVIDED PLASTIC BUCKET   D. CART
_____ 2. FILL BOTH SIDES OF DIVIDED BUCKET ½ FULL OF CLEAN WATER.
_____ 3. REMOVE CHALK AND ERASERS FROM CHALK TRAY.
_____ 4. ERASE ANY WRITING FROM BOARD.
_____ 5. VACUUM FRAME AND TRAY OF BOARD.
_____ 6. VACUUM ENTIRE FACE OF BOARD.
_____ 7. DIP CLOTH IN WATER IN ONE SIDE OF BUCKET. WRING CLOTH
                   DRY AND WIPE ENTIRE FACE OF BOARD AND ALLOW TO DRY.
_____ 8. DIP ANOTHER CLOTH IN SECOND SIDE OF BUCKET. WRING CLOTH
                   DRY AND RINSE ENTIRE FACE OF BOARD.
_____ 9. WHILE WAITING FOR BOARD TO DRY, REMOVE WAND FROM
                   VACUUM CLEANER AND VACUUM ALL ERASERS.
_____ 10. IF BOARD IS STREAKED, WASH AGAIN.
_____ 11. REPLACE CHALK AND ERASERS IN TRAY OF CHALK BOARD.
_____ 12. GO ON TO THE NEXT BOARD TO BE CLEANED OR REPORT TO
                    SUPERVISOR WHEN TASK IS COMPLETED.

WORKS AT STEADY PACE:

EXCESSIVE TALKING - NO. TIMES_____   TIME FINISHED_____

LEAVING WORK AREA - NO. TIMES_____   TIME STARTED_____

IDLE - NUMBER TIMES_____   TOTAL TIME_____

                                        CODE 139

                                        TOKENS_____

                                        PERCENTAGE_____%

CENTER FOR DEVELOPMENTAL AND LEARNING DISORDERS
TOKEN ECONOMY

11/15/72

NAME_____

DATE_____

LACING COIN PURSE

TOKEN VALUE 3 per ½ hour

YES   NO

_____ 1. OBTAIN PROPER KIT.

_____ 2. OBTAIN LACING NEEDLE.

_____ 3. PLACE LACING LEATHER INTO NEEDLE.

_____ 4. ASSEMBLE PIECES IN DESIGNATED LOCATION.

_____ 5. BEGIN TO LACE AT DESIGNATED LOCATION.

_____ 6. LACE PROJECT USING WHIP STITCH.

_____ 7. SEE THAT LACING IS NOT TWISTED.

_____ 8. WHEN FINISHED RETURN ALL TOOLS TO DESIGNATED PLACE.

_____ 9. CLEAN UP WORK AREA.

_____ 10. INFORM SUPERVISOR WHEN JOB IS FINISHED.

WORKS AT STEADY PACE:

EXCESSIVE TALKING - NO. TIMES _____   TIME FINISHED _____

LEAVING WORK AREA - NO. TIMES _____   TIME STARTED _____

IDLE - NUMBER TIMES _____   TOTAL TIME _____

CODE 088

TOKENS _____

PERCENTAGE _____ %

CENTER FOR DEVELOPMENTAL AND LEARNING DISORDERS

TOKEN ECONOMY

2/15/72   NAME_____

DATE_____

CLEANING ALL BLINDS IN ADL (7 SETS)

TOKEN VALUE 6

YES   NO

_____   1. ASSEMBLE SUPPLIES:
                      A. CLOTHS
                      B. POLISH
_____   2. SPRAY ONE OR TWO SLATS WITH POLISH. WIPE WITH DRY CLOTH.
_____   3. REPEAT STEP 2 UNTIL ALL BLINDS ARE CLEAN.
_____   4. REPLACE SUPPLIES.
_____   5. INFORM SUPERVISOR WHEN FINISHED.

WORKS AT STEADY PACE:

EXCESSIVE TALKING - NO. TIMES _____   TIME FINISHED_____

LEAVING WORK AREA - NO. TIMES _____   TIME STARTED _____

IDLE - NUMBER TIMES _____   TOTAL TIME _____

CODE   023

TOKENS _____

PERCENTAGE _____%

CENTER FOR DEVELOPMENTAL AND LEARNING DISORDERS

TOKEN ECONOMY

9/20/72   NAME_____

                                           DATE_____

EMPTYING AND WASHING TRASH CANS

TOKEN VALUE 3 per ½ hour

YES   NO

_____ 1. ASSEMBLE TRASH CANS AND SUPPLIES AND TAKE TO WORK AREA:
                A. ABRASIVE CLEANER   D. LINERS
                B. DISINFECTANT   E. SCRUB BRUSH
                C. CLOTHS FOR DRYING

_____ 2. TAKE TRASH CANS AND EMPTY INTO ONE.

_____ 3. PUT FULL ONE BY DOOR.

_____ 4. WASH AND SCRUB TRASH CAN WITH ABRASIVE CLEANER AND
               DISINFECTANT INSIDE AND OUT.

_____ 5. RINSE TRASH CANS.

_____ 6. DRY AND LINE TRASH CANS AND REPLACE THEM IN THE WORK
               AREAS.

_____ 7. CLEAN WORK AREA AND REPLACE ALL SUPPLIES.

_____ 8. INFORM SUPERVISOR WHEN TASK IS COMPLETED.

WORKS AT STEADY PACE:

  EXCESSIVE TALKING - NO. TIMES_____   TIME FINISHED_____

  LEAVING WORK AREA - NO. TIMES_____   TIME STARTED_____

  IDLE - NUMBER TIMES_____   TOTAL TIME_____

CODE   160

TOKENS_____

PERCENTAGE_____%

CENTER FOR DEVELOPMENTAL AND LEARNING DISORDERS

TOKEN ECONOMY

11/17/72

NAME_____

DATE_____

WET MOPPING

TOKEN VALUE 3 per ½ hour

YES   NO

_____ 1. ASSEMBLE SUPPLIES AND EQUIPMENT:
   A. MOP   C. BUCKET
   B. SOAP

_____ 2. FILL BUCKET HALF FULL OF WARM WATER.

_____ 3. PUT THE CORRECT MEASURE (FOLLOW DIRECTIONS ON SOAP CONTAINER) INTO BUCKET.

_____ 4. DAMPEN MOP.

_____ 5. SQUEEZE MOP OUT DRY.

_____ 6. GO OVER AREA TO BE CLEANED, WITH FIGURE 8 MOTIONS, IN SMALL SECTIONS UNTIL AREA HAS BEEN COMPLETELY MOPPED. WALK BACKWARDS SO AS NOT TO TRACK OVER MOPPED AREA.

_____ 7. RINSE MOP AND BUCKET.

_____ 8. FILL BUCKET HALF FULL OF COOL WATER.

_____ 9. DAMPEN MOP IN RINSE WATER AND WRING OUT DRY.

_____ 10. GO OVER FLOOR WITH FIGURE 8 MOTIONS RINSING SMALL SECTIONS AT A TIME UNTIL AREA HAS BEEN COMPLETELY RINSED.

_____ 11. RINSE OUT BUCKET AND MOP.

_____ 12. PUT AWAY SUPPLIES AND EQUIPMENT.

_____ 13. INFORM SUPERVISOR WHEN FINISHED.

WORKS AT STEADY PACE:

EXCESSIVE TALKING - NO. TIMES _____   TIME FINISHED _____

LEAVING WORK AREA - NO. TIMES _____   TIME STARTED _____

IDLE - NUMBER TIMES _____   TOTAL TIME _____

CODE 038

TOKENS _____

PERCENTAGE _____ %

CENTER FOR DEVELOPMENTAL AND LEARNING DISORDERS

TOKEN ECONOMY

11/2/72   NAME_____

DATE_____

HOLE PUNCHING

TOKEN VALUE 3 per ½ hour

YES   NO

_____ 1. GET HOLE PUNCHER FROM PRINT SHOP.

_____ 2. TAKE FIVE SHEETS OF PAPER MAKING ALL EDGES EVEN.

_____ 3. PLACE STACK OF PAPER IN GUIDES TO BE PUNCHED.

_____ 4. PUNCH HOLES ON THE OUTSIDE EDGE OF PAPERS IN
               APPROPRIATE PLACE AS INDICATED BY THE GUIDES.

_____ 5. REPEAT STEPS 2, 3 AND 4 UNTIL HOLES HAVE BEEN PUNCHED IN
               THE ASSIGNED STACK OF PAPER.

_____ 6. CLEAN UP WORK AREA.

_____ 7. INFORM SUPERVISOR WHEN TASK IS FINISHED.

WORKS AT STEADY PACE:

EXCESSIVE TALKING - NO. TIMES _____   TIME FINISHED_____

LEAVING WORK AREA - NO. TIMES _____   TIME STARTED_____

IDLE - NUMBER TIMES _____   TOTAL TIME_____

CODE 148

TOKENS _____

PERCENTAGE _____%

CENTER FOR DEVELOPMENTAL AND LEARNING DISORDERS

TOKEN ECONOMY

1/5/72   NAME_____

                          DATE_____

LACING COMB CASE

TOKEN VALUE 3 per ½ hour

YES   NO   *NOTE: FILL IN STITCH TO BE USED
_____   BEFORE STUDENT-CLIENT BEGINS
                                       WORKING ON JOB DESCRIPTION.
_____ 1. GET PROPER KIT.

_____ 2. GET LACING NEEDLE.

_____ 3. PLACE LACING LEATHER INTO NEEDLE.

_____ 4. PLACE PIECES TO BE ASSEMBLED OVER EACH OTHER IN PROPER
               ALIGNMENT.

_____ 5. BEGIN TO LACE AT THE RIGHT PLACE.

_____ 6. LACE PROJECT USING _____* STITCH.

_____ 7. DO NOT TWIST LACING.

_____ 8. WHEN FINISHED RETURN ALL TOOLS TO PROPER PLACE.

_____ 9. CLEAN UP WORK AREA.

_____ 10. INFORM SUPERVISOR WHEN JOB IS FINISHED.

WORKS AT STEADY PACE:

EXCESSIVE TALKING - NO. TIMES _____   TIME FINISHED _____

LEAVING WORK AREA - NO. TIMES _____   TIME STARTED _____

IDLE - NUMBER TIMES _____   TOTAL TIME _____

_____

CODE   089

TOKENS _____

PERCENTAGE _____ %

_____

CENTER FOR DEVELOPMENTAL AND LEARNING DISORDERS

TOKEN ECONOMY

11/17/72

NAME_____

DATE_____

CLEANING DOUBLE KITCHEN SINKS

TOKEN VALUE 3 per ½ hour

YES   NO

_____ 1. ASSEMBLE SUPPLIES AND EQUIPMENT:
    A. CLEANSER
    B. SPONGE
    C. CLOTH

_____ 2. DAMPEN SPONGE AND SQUEEZE OUT INTO BOTH SINKS SO THAT BOTH SINKS ARE DAMPENED.

_____ 3. SPRINKLE CLEANSER LIGHTLY OVER SINK SURFACE.

_____ 4. SCRUB WITH SPONGE TO REMOVE FILM, STREAKS OR STAINS.

_____ 5. CLEAN AND RINSE SPONGE AND SINK.

_____ 6. DRY SINK WITH CLOTH.

_____ 7. WIPE OFF BACK OF SINK BEHIND FAUCETS.

_____ 8. WIPE WATER SPOTS OFF FAUCETS.

_____ 9. WIPE OFF DISH DRAIN AND TRAY; WIPE UNDER DRAIN TRAY.

_____ 10. PUT CLEANING SUPPLIES AWAY.

_____ 11. INFORM SUPERVISOR WHEN FINISHED.

WORKS AT STEADY PACE:

EXCESSIVE TALKING - NO. TIMES_____   TIME FINISHED_____

LEAVING WORK AREA - NO. TIMES_____   TIME STARTED_____

IDLE - NUMBER TIMES_____   TOTAL TIME_____

CODE 027

TOKENS_____

PERCENTAGE_____%

CENTER FOR DEVELOPMENTAL AND LEARNING DISORDERS

TOKEN ECONOMY

10/13/72

NAME_____

DATE_____

HAND SANDING

TOKEN VALUE 3 per ½ hour

YES   NO

_____ 1. SELECT PROPER GRIT PAPER.

_____ 2. PLACE WOOD IN A FIXED POSITION.

_____ 3. PROCEED TO SAND USING GENTLE PRESSURE FOLLOWING GRAIN.

_____ 4. PUSH SANDPAPER EVENLY ACROSS OBJECT.

_____ 5. DISCARD USED SANDPAPER. REPLACE REUSABLE SANDPAPER IN
                 DESIGNATED PLACE.

_____ 6. REPLACE WOOD IN PROPER PLACE.

_____ 7. CLEAN WORK AREA.

_____ 8. INFORM SUPERVISOR WHEN TASK IS FINISHED.

WORKS AT STEADY PACE:

EXCESSIVE TALKING - NO. TIMES _____   TIME FINISHED _____

LEAVING WORK AREA - NO. TIMES _____   TIME STARTED _____

IDLE - NUMBER TIMES _____   TOTAL TIME _____

CODE 114

TOKENS _____

PERCENTAGE _____ %

CENTER FOR DEVELOPMENTAL AND LEARNING DISORDERS

TOKEN ECONOMY

NAME_____

DATE_____

DUST MOPPING

TOKEN VALUE 2

YES   NO

_____ 1. ASSEMBLE MATERIALS:
- A. DUST MOPPING TOOL   D. COUNTER BRUSH
- B. DUST MOP COVER   E. DUSTPAN
- C. PUTTY KNIFE

_____ 2. PROCEED TO WORK AREA. TRAVEL TO WORK AREA ON THE RIGHT SIDE OF THE HALL.

_____ 3. USING A FIGURE "8" MOTION, SWEEP ENTIRE AREA WITHOUT LIFTING DUST MOP.

_____ 4. USING COUNTER BRUSH, SWEEP DUST INTO DUSTPAN.

_____ 5. SWEEP ALL HARD-TO-REACH CORNERS WITH COUNTER BRUSH.

_____ 6. REMOVE ALL CHEWING GUM AND OTHER GUMMY SUBSTANCES WITH PUTTY KNIFE (BEING CAREFUL NOT TO CUT FLOOR).

_____ 7. SHAKE COUNTER BRUSH AND SWEEPING TOOL OVER THE NEAREST LARGE TRASH CONTAINER.

_____ 8. RETURN SWEEPING SUPPLIES TO SUPPLY ROOM AND PLACE AGAINST THE WALL.

_____ 9. CLEAN DUSTPAN AND COUNTER BRUSH WITHOUT USING WATER ON COUNTER BRUSH.

_____ 10. INFORM SUPERVISOR WHEN TASK IS COMPLETED.

WORKS AT STEADY PACE:

EXCESSIVE TALKING - NO. TIMES_____   TIME FINISHED _____

LEAVING WORK AREA - NO. TIMES_____   TIME STARTED _____

IDLE - NUMBER TIMES _____   TOTAL TIME _____

CODE 124

TOKENS _____

PERCENTAGE _____%

CENTER FOR DEVELOPMENTAL AND LEARNING DISORDERS

TOKEN ECONOMY

2/10/72

NAME_____

DATE_____

COLLATING BULLETINS

TOKEN VALUE 3 per ½ hour

YES   NO

_____ 1. PICK UP SHEETS OF PAPER AND PLACE THEM IN DESIGNATED
               ORDER.

_____ 2. PLACE COLLATED BULLETINS IN DESIGNATED PLACE TO BE
               STAPLED.

WORKS AT STEADY PACE:

EXCESSIVE TALKING - NO. TIMES _____   TIME FINISHED _____

LEAVING WORK AREA - NO. TIMES _____   TIME STARTED _____

IDLE - NUMBER TIMES _____   TOTAL TIME _____

CODE 073

TOKENS _____

PERCENTAGE _____ %

CENTER FOR DEVELOPMENTAL AND LEARNING DISORDERS

TOKEN ECONOMY

11/17/72

NAME_____

DATE_____

CLEANING TOILET

TOKEN VALUE 3 per ½ hour

YES   NO

_____ 1. ASSEMBLE SUPPLIES:
           A. SPONGE   C. CLEANSER
           B. TOILET BRUSH

_____ 2. SPRINKLE CLEANSER INSIDE TOILET BOWL.

_____ 3. SCRUB TOILET BOWL WITH BRUSH.

_____ 4. DAMPEN SPONGE.

_____ 5. SPRINKLE CLEANSER ON SPONGE.

_____ 6. SCRUB ENTIRE SURFACE OF TOILET PAYING CLOSE ATTENTION
           TO TOILET SEAT.

_____ 7. RINSE SPONGE AND BRUSH.

_____ 8. RINSE OFF ENTIRE SURFACE OF TOILET WITH CLEAN DAMP
           SPONGE.

_____ 9. FLUSH TOILET.

_____ 10. RINSE SPONGE.

_____ 11. REPLACE SUPPLIES.

_____ 12. INFORM SUPERVISOR WHEN TASK IS COMPLETED.

WORKS AT STEADY PACE:

EXCESSIVE TALKING - NO. TIMES _____   TIME FINISHED _____

LEAVING WORK AREA - NO. TIMES _____   TIME STARTED _____

IDLE - NUMBER TIMES _____   TOTAL TIME _____

CODE 028

TOKENS _____

PERCENTAGE _____%

CENTER FOR DEVELOPMENTAL AND LEARNING DISORDERS

TOKEN ECONOMY

1/12/72   NAME_____

                                           DATE_____

CLEAN-UP EVALUATION AND ADJUSTMENT LABORATORY

TOKEN VALUE 3 per ½ hour

YES   NO

_____ 1. STORE ALL HAND TOOLS IN DESIGNATED PLACE.

_____ 2. DUST MACHINES AND FLAT SURFACES.

_____ 3. SWEEP FLOORS PAYING CLOSE ATTENTION TO CORNERS, UNDER
                  TABLES AND UNDER CHAIRS.

_____ 4. USE DUST MOP AFTER SWEEPING.

_____ 5. PICK UP TRASH WITH VACUUM CLEANER.

_____ 6. RETURN BROOM AND MOP WITH OTHER CLEANING SUPPLIES TO
                  DESIGNATED PLACE.

_____ 7. INFORM SUPERVISOR WHEN FINISHED.

WORKS AT STEADY PACE:

   EXCESSIVE TALKING - NO. TIMES _____   TIME FINISHED _____

   LEAVING WORK AREA - NO. TIMES _____   TIME STARTED _____

   IDLE - NUMBER TIMES _____   TOTAL TIME _____

                          _____

                          CODE   072

                          TOKENS _____

                          PERCENTAGE _____%

                          _____

CENTER FOR DEVELOPMENTAL AND LEARNING DISORDERS

TOKEN ECONOMY

10/22/71   NAME_____

                                            DATE_____

CLEANING BATHTUB

TOKEN VALUE 1

YES   NO

_____ 1. ASSEMBLE SUPPLIES:

        A.SPONGE   C. DRY CLOTHS

        B. CLEANSER   D. POLISH

_____ 2. TURN ON WATER IN TUB AND MOISTEN THE TUB AND SPONGE.

_____ 3. SPRINKLE CLEANING AGENT OVER TUB AND FAUCETS.

_____ 4. RUB ENTIRE SURFACE OF TUB AND FAUCETS WITH DAMP SPONGE MAKING SURE TO REMOVE ALL STAINS AND DIRT.

_____ 5. RINSE ENTIRE SURFACE OF TUB AND FAUCETS GETTING RID OF ALL GRIT.

_____ 6. POLISH CHROME FIXTURES WITH DRY CLOTH LEAVING NO STREAKS.

_____ 7. RINSE SPONGE. POLISH OUTSIDE OF TUB WITH POLISH, RUBBING TO REMOVE ANY STREAKS.

_____ 8. PUT SUPPLIES IN DESIGNATED PLACE.

_____ 9. INFORM SUPERVISOR WHEN TASK IS COMPLETED.

WORKS AT STEADY PACE:

    EXCESSIVE TALKING - NO. TIMES_____   TIME FINISHED_____

    LEAVING WORK AREA - NO. TIMES_____   TIME STARTED_____

    IDLE - NUMBER TIMES_____   TOTAL TIME_____

                                         CODE 022

                                         TOKENS_____

                                         PERCENTAGE_____%

CENTER FOR DEVELOPMENTAL AND LEARNING DISORDERS

TOKEN ECONOMY

11/15/72

NAME_____

DATE_____

LEATHER PRACTICE PIECES

TOKEN VALUE 3 per ½ hour

YES   NO

_____ 1. GET LEATHER PRACTICE PIECE.

_____ 2. DRAW ASSIGNED PATTERN ON TRACING PAPER.

_____ 3. DAMPEN LEATHER ON BOTH SIDES.

_____ 4. TRACE PATTERN ONTO LEATHER USING STYLUS.

_____ 5. CUT PATTERN INTO LEATHER USING SWIREL KNIFE.

_____ 6. USE APPROPRIATE TOOLS TO BRING OUT PATTERN.

_____ 7. RETURN ALL TOOLS TO DESIGNATED PLACE.

_____ 8. CLEAN UP WORK AREA.

_____ 9. INFORM SUPERVISOR WHEN JOB IS FINISHED.

WORKS AT STEADY PACE:

EXCESSIVE TALKING - NO. TIMES _____   TIME FINISHED_____

LEAVING WORK AREA - NO. TIMES _____   TIME STARTED_____

IDLE - NUMBER TIMES _____   TOTAL TIME_____

CODE 092

TOKENS_____

PERCENTAGE_____%

CENTER FOR DEVELOPMENTAL AND LEARNING DISORDERS

TOKEN ECONOMY

2/22/72

NAME_____

DATE_____

WASHING HAIR

TOKEN VALUE 2*

YES   NO

_____   1. ASSEMBLE SUPPLIES:

      A. SHAMPOO   C. SHAMPOO CAPE

      B. CREAM RINSE   D. TOWEL

_____   2. PUT ON SHAMPOO CAPE.

_____   3. TURN ON WATER AND ADJUST TO A WARM, COMFORTABLE TEMPERATURE.

_____   4. PLACE HEAD IN SINK AND WET HAIR WITH WARM WATER.

_____   5. FILL PALM OF HAND WITH SHAMPOO AND RUB INTO HAIR WORKING UP A LATHER.

_____   6. RUB SHAMPOO INTO HAIR MAKING SURE TO SCRUB THE SCALP WITH FINGER TIPS.

_____   7. RINSE ALL SHAMPOO FROM HAIR UNTIL HAIR SQUEAKS WHEN RUBBED.

_____   8. REPEAT STEPS 4, 5, AND 6.

_____   9. FILL PALM OF HAND WITH CREAM RINSE. APPLY TO HAIR AND RUB OVER ENTIRE SURFACE OF SCALP.

_____   10. RINSE HAIR THREE TIMES.

_____   11. TOWEL HAIR DRY.

_____   12. RETURN SUPPLIES TO CABINET.

_____   13. CLEAN WORK AREA.

_____   14. INFORM SUPERVISOR WHEN TASK IS FINISHED AND GO TO ROLL HAIR OR DRY HAIR.

WORKS AT STEADY PACE:

    EXCESSIVE TALKING - NO. TIMES_____   TIME FINISHED_____

    LEAVING WORK AREA - NO. TIMES_____   TOTAL TIME_____

    IDLE - NUMBER TIMES_____

*ONLY TO APPLY TO A CLIENT WITH A "NO" CHECK IN GROOMING ON CLEAN HAIR. OTHER CLIENTS PAY TO WASH HAIR AS A CONTINGENCY.

CODE 039

TOKENS_____

PERCENTAGE_____%

CENTER FOR DEVELOPMENTAL AND LEARNING DISORDERS

TOKEN ECONOMY

6/22/72   NAME_____

DATE_____

SETTING TABLE

TOKEN VALUE 3

<u>YES   NO</u>

_____ 1. ASSEMBLE SUPPLIES AND EQUIPMENT: (5 MINUTES)
   A. TABLE CLOTH   E. WATER GLASS
   B. NAPKIN   F. KNIFE
   C. DINNER FORK   G. SPOON
   D. PLATE   H. BREAD AND BUTTER PLATE
                        (IF NECESSARY)

_____ 2. PLACE TABLE CLOTH ON TABLE.

_____ 3. PLACE PLATE DIRECTLY IN FRONT OF CHAIR. (REMEMBER TO
   LINE SERVICE UP APPROXIMATELY ONE INCH FROM TABLE EDGE.)

_____ 4. PLACE KNIFE AT THE RIGHT OF THE PLATE WITH THE CUTTING
   EDGE TOWARD THE PLATE.

_____ 5. PLACE SPOON AT THE RIGHT OF THE KNIFE.

_____ 6. PLACE WATER GLASS AT THE TIP OF THE KNIFE.

_____ 7. PLACE FORK AT THE LEFT OF THE PLATE, TINES TURNED UP.

_____ 8. PLACE BREAD AND BUTTER PLATE AT THE TIP OF THE FORK.

_____ 9. PLACE NAPKIN AT THE LEFT OF THE FORK WITH THE HEM AND
   SELVAGED EDGE PARALLEL TO THE EDGE OF THE TABLE AND
   THE FORK.

_____ 10. INFORM SUPERVISOR WHEN JOB IS COMPLETED.

WORKS AT STEADY PACE:

EXCESSIVE TALKING - NO. TIMES _____   TIME FINISHED _____

LEAVING WORK AREA - NO. TIMES _____   TIME STARTED _____

IDLE - NUMBER TIMES _____   TOTAL TIME _____

CODE <u>162</u>

TOKENS _____

PERCENTAGE _____ %

CENTER FOR DEVELOPMENTAL AND LEARNING DISORDERS

TOKEN ECONOMY

2/16/72

NAME_____

DATE_____

DRYING HAIR

TOKEN VALUE 1*

YES   NO

_____ 1. SELECT (1) EXTRA WARM, OR (2) HOT DRYING TEMPERATURE ON DIAL ON HAIR DRYER.

_____ 2. SELECT LENGTH OF TIME TO DRY ON DIAL ON HAIR DRYER.

_____ 3. SIT DOWN IN CHAIR.

_____ 4. PULL HOOD DOWN OVER HAIR.

_____ 5. WHEN DRYER CUTS OFF, RAISE HOOD.

_____ 6. CHECK TO MAKE SURE HAIR IS DRY. IF NOT, REPEAT STEPS 2-6.

_____ 7. CLEAN WORK AREA.

_____ 8. INFORM SUPERVISOR WHEN TASK IS COMPLETED.

WORKS AT STEADY PACE:

EXCESSIVE TALKING - NO. TIMES _____   TIME FINISHED _____

LEAVING WORK AREA - NO. TIMES _____   TIME STARTED _____

IDLE - NUMBER TIMES _____   TOTAL TIME _____

*ONLY TO APPLY TO SOMEONE WITH A "NO" CHECK IN GROOMING ON CLEAN HAIR.

CODE 041

TOKENS _____

PERCENTAGE _____ %

CENTER FOR DEVELOPMENTAL AND LEARNING DISORDERS

TOKEN ECONOMY

2/29/72   NAME_____

                                 DATE_____

COMBING HAIR

TOKEN VALUE 2*

YES   NO
_____

_____ 1. ASSEMBLE SUPPLIES:
               (A) BRUSH
               (B) COMB
               (C) HAIR SPRAY OR HAIRDRESSING

_____ 2. REMOVE HAIRNET, ROLLERS, PINS AND CLIPS FROM HAIR IF HAIR
               HAS BEEN ROLLED.

_____ 3. HEAT COMB IF HOT COMB IS USED.

_____ 4. BRUSH HAIR STARTING AT THE SCALP AND WORKING TOWARD
               THE ENDS.

_____ 5. COMB HAIR INTO DESIRED STYLE USING HAIRDRESSING IF
               NEEDED. IF HOT COMB IS USED, ALLOW THE HAIR TO COOL
               BEFORE BRUSHING HAIR INTO DESIRED STYLE.

_____ 6. SPRAY HAIR.

_____ 7. PLACE COMB AND BRUSH USED IN PROPER PLACE TO BE
               CLEANED.

_____ 8. RETURN SUPPLIES AND OTHER HAIR GROOMING AIDS TO
               STORAGE AREA.

_____ 9. INFORM SUPERVISOR WHEN TASK IS COMPLETED.

WORKS AT STEADY PACE:

    EXCESSIVE TALKING - NO. TIMES _____   TIME FINISHED _____

    LEAVING WORK AREA - NO. TIMES _____   TIME STARTED _____

    IDLE - NUMBER TIMES _____   TOTAL TIME _____

*ONLY TO APPLY TO SOMEONE WITH A
"NO" CHECK ON GROOMING (HAIR
NEATLY COMBED).

                    _____

                    CODE   042

                    TOKENS _____

                    PERCENTAGE _____%

                    _____

CENTER FOR DEVELOPMENTAL AND LEARNING DISORDERS

TOKEN ECONOMY

3/2/72

NAME_____

DATE_____

DRYING HAIR WITH ELECTRIC COMB OR BRUSH

TOKEN VALUE 1*

YES   NO
‾‾‾‾‾‾‾‾‾‾‾‾

_____ 1. ASSEMBLE SUPPLIES:
                  A. COMB
                  B. BRUSH SET
                  C. ATTACHMENTS

_____ 2. BRUSH HAIR MAKING SURE YOU BRUSH THE UNDERNEATH SIDE
                UNTIL HAIR IS DRY.

_____ 3. REMOVE ATTACHMENT USED AND REMOVE ANY HAIR LEFT ON IT.

_____ 4. RETURN SUPPLIES TO DRAWER.

_____ 5. CLEAN WORK AREA.

_____ 6. INFORM SUPERVISOR WHEN TASK IS COMPLETED.

WORKS AT STEADY PACE:

EXCESSIVE TALKING - NO. TIMES_____   TIME FINISHED_____

LEAVING WORK AREA - NO. TIMES_____   TIME STARTED_____

IDLE - NUMBER TIMES_____   TOTAL TIME_____

*ONLY TO APPLY TO SOMEONE WITH A
"NO" CHECK IN GROOMING (CLEAN
HAIR).

_____

CODE 063

TOKENS_____

PERCENTAGE_____%

_____

CENTER FOR DEVELOPMENTAL AND LEARNING DISORDERS

TOKEN ECONOMY

11/13/72

NAME_____

DATE_____

STAPLING

TOKEN VALUE 3 per ½ hour

YES   NO

_____ 1. STACK PAPERS MAKING ALL EDGES EVEN.

_____ 2. PLACE STACKS OF PAPER IN GUIDES TO BE STAPLED.

_____ 3. STAPLE OUTSIDE EDGE OF PAPERS IN APPROPRIATE PLACE AS INDICATED BY THE GUIDES.

_____ 4. PUT STAPLERS IN PROPER PLACE IN PRINT LAB.

WORKS AT STEADY PACE:

EXCESSIVE TALKING - NO. TIMES _____   TIME FINISHED _____

LEAVING WORK AREA - NO. TIMES _____   TIME STARTED _____

IDLE - NUMBER TIMES _____   TOTAL TIME _____

CODE 149

TOKENS _____

PERCENTAGE _____%

CENTER FOR DEVELOPMENTAL AND LEARNING DISORDERS

TOKEN ECONOMY

10/16/72

NAME_____

DATE_____

EMPTYING VACUUM CLEANER

TOKEN VALUE 1

YES   NO

_____ 1. UNPLUG MACHINE FROM WALL OUTLET.

_____ 2. RELEASE SNAP RING.

_____ 3. REMOVE SNAP RING FROM MACHINE.

_____ 4. LIFT UP TOP AND PLACE ON FLOOR.

_____ 5. REMOVE CLOTH COVER AND LIGHTLY HIT WALLS IN DRUM TO REMOVE DUST.

_____ 6. TAKE MACHINE TO GROUND FLOOR AND EMPTY DUST INTO GARBAGE CONTAINERS.

_____ 7. RETURN MACHINE TO SHOP.

_____ 8. REPLACE CLOTH COVER.

_____ 9. REPLACE MACHINE TOP.

_____ 10. REPLACE SNAP RING.

_____ 11. REPLUG AND TEST MACHINE.

_____ 12. INFORM SUPERVISOR WHEN JOB IS FINISHED.

WORKS AT STEADY PACE:

EXCESSIVE TALKING - NO. TIMES _____   TIME FINISHED _____

LEAVING WORK AREA - NO. TIMES _____   TIME STARTED _____

IDLE - NUMBER TIMES _____   TOTAL TIME _____

CODE 125

TOKENS _____

PERCENTAGE _____ %

CENTER FOR DEVELOPMENTAL AND LEARNING DISORDERS

TOKEN ECONOMY

NAME_____

WORK AREA_____   DATE_____

HAND DUSTING

TOKEN VALUE 4

YES   NO

_____   1. ASSEMBLE SUPPLIES:
              A. DUST RAGS (CLEAN)

_____   2. DUST ALL PLACES THAT YOU CAN REACH. (NOT WALLS OR
              FLOORS)

_____   3. USE A NEW RAG FOR EACH ROOM OR HALL TO BE DUSTED.

_____   4. PLACE RAGS IN TRASH CAN WHEN YOU MOVE TO NEXT ROOM.

_____   5. INFORM SUPERVISOR WHEN JOB IS COMPLETED.

WORKS AT STEADY PACE:

EXCESSIVE TALKING - NO. TIMES _____   TIME FINISHED _____

LEAVING WORK AREA - NO. TIMES _____   TIME STARTED _____

IDLE - NUMBER TIMES _____   TOTAL TIME _____

CODE 136

TOKENS _____

PERCENTAGE _____%

APPENDIX B

EXAMPLES OF
GREEN LEVEL JOB DESCRIPTIONS

CENTER FOR DEVELOPMENTAL AND LEARNING DISORDERS
TOKEN ECONOMY

2/15/72

NAME_____

DATE_____

BED MAKING

TOKEN VALUE 1

YES   NO

_____ 1. ASSEMBLE SUPPLIES:
      A. BOTTOM SHEET   C. PILLOW CASES
      B. TOP SHEET

_____ 2. REMOVE USED SHEETS, PILLOW CASES AND SPREAD FROM BED.

_____ 3. FOLD SPREAD AND PLACE ON A CHAIR.

_____ 4. FIT BOTTOM SHEET OVER THE MATTRESS, FOLDING CORNERS UNDER THE MATTRESS IF SHEET IS NOT FITTED.

_____ 5. PUT TOP SHEET ON BED. TUCK IN BOTTOM CORNERS.

_____ 6. PUT SPREAD ON BED WITH BOTH SIDES AND BOTTOM EDGE THE SAME DISTANCE FROM THE FLOOR.

_____ 7. FOLD BACK APPROXIMATELY 1 AND $\frac{1}{2}$ FEET (18 INCHES) OF THE SPREAD.

_____ 8. FLUFF PILLOWS.

_____ 9. PLACE PILLOWS IN PILLOW CASES.

_____ 10. PUT PILLOWS AT THE TOP OF THE BED.

_____ 11. LAY TOP EDGE OF SPREAD OVER PILLOWS. TUCK SPREAD UNDER AND BEHIND PILLOWS.

_____ 12. PUT DIRTY SHEETS AND PILLOW CASES IN LAUNDRY.

_____ 13. INFORM SUPERVISOR WHEN TASK IS COMPLETED.

WORKS AT STEADY PACE:

EXCESSIVE TALKING - NO. TIMES _____   TIME FINISHED_____

LEAVING WORK AREA - NO. TIMES _____   TIME STARTED_____

IDLE - NUMBER TIMES _____   TOTAL TIME_____

CODE 020

TOKENS _____

PERCENTAGE _____%

152

CENTER FOR DEVELOPMENTAL AND LEARNING DISORDERS
TOKEN ECONOMY

2/3/72

NAME_____

DATE_____

CHECKING ABSENTEES

TOKEN VALUE 5
TIME 45 MINUTES

YES   NO

_____ 1. REPORT TO THE EVALUATION AND ADJUSTMENT LAB BY
              8:30 A.M.

_____ 2. PULL ABSENTEE CARDS AT 8:40 A.M.

_____ 3. CHECK TIME CARDS TO SEE IF CARD HAS BEEN PUNCHED FOR THE
              DAY. IF IT HAS, THE CARD IS TO BE RETURNED TO THE CORRECT
              RACK.

_____ 4. COUNT NUMBER PRESENT FOR MEAL COUNT.
                 A. NUMBER FREE LUNCHES FIGURED CORRECTLY
                 B. NUMBER PAID LUNCHES FIGURED CORRECTLY
                 C. NUMBER REDUCED LUNCHES FIGURED CORRECTLY
                 D. LUNCHES TOTALED CORRECTLY

_____ 5. FILL OUT MEAL COUNT FORM CORRECTLY.

_____ 6. TYPE STENCIL OF ABSENTEES CORRECTLY.
                 A. PROPER HEADING AND DATE
                 B. BLOCK MARGIN
                 C. NAMES SPELLED AS THEY ARE ON THE CARDS

           *IF A PERSON IS LATE AND HIS NAME HAS ALREADY BEEN TYPED ON
           THE STENCIL, MAKE A LINE THROUGH HIS NAME ON THE STENCIL.
           IF THE STENCIL HAS ALREADY BEEN RUN, MAKE ONE LINE
           THROUGH THAT PERSON'S NAME ON EACH SHEET.

_____ 7. RUN STENCIL ON WHITE PAPER.

_____ 8. DELIVER ABSENTEE LIST TO STAFF.

_____ 9. DELIVER MEAL COUNT FORM TO PERSON IN ROOM 611.

_____ 10. REPORT BACK TO EVALUATION AND ADJUSTMENT LAB BY
              9:15 A.M.

_____

CODE   184

TOKENS _____

PERCENTAGE _____%

_____

CENTER FOR DEVELOPMENTAL AND LEARNING DISORDERS
TOKEN ECONOMY

7/10/72

NAME_____

DATE_____

COPY MACHINE OPERATOR

TOKEN VALUE 3 per ½ hour

YES   NO

_____ 1. READ REQUEST FORM TO DETERMINE TOTAL NUMBER OF STENCILS REQUESTED.

_____ 2. RAISE PLASTIC COVER. CHECK PLASTIC CARRIAGE TO BE SURE NO COPIES ARE LEFT IN MACHINE.

_____ 3. CHECK PAPER TO BE COPIED FOR INK SPOTS.

_____ 4. USE WHITE CORRECTION FLUID TO COVER ALL INK SPOTS.

_____ 5. RELEASE PLASTIC BINDER BY TURNING KNOB ON LEFT SIDE OF CYLINDER.

_____ 6. PLACE COPY IN PLASTIC GUIDE USING ZEROS AT THE TOP AS A GUIDE TO KEEP THE PAPER STRAIGHT.

_____ 7. FASTEN PLASTIC COVER BACK TO CYLINDER.

_____ 8. REMOVE STENCIL FROM PACK AND RELEASE BINDER ON PHOTO-CELL CYLINDER BY TURNING KNOB ON RIGHT SIDE OF CYLINDER.

_____ 9. PLACE STENCIL FROM PACK ON CYLINDER USING INSIDE GUIDELINES TO KEEP STRAIGHT.

_____ 10. BRING BOTTOM OF STENCIL BACK THROUGH TO BOTTOM EDGE OF CYLINDER BINDER FOR ALIGNMENT.

_____ 11. FASTEN BINDER BACK TO CYLINDER.

_____ 12. CLOSE PLASTIC COVER.

_____ 13. PUSH ON-OFF SWITCH TO "ON;" LET MACHINE WARM UP UNTIL PHOTO-CELL LIGHT COMES ON.

_____ 14. PUSH CYLINDER TO FAR LEFT.

_____ 15. PULL START BUTTON TO "ON" POSITION.

_____ 16. WHEN MACHINE CUTS OFF AUTOMATICALLY, REMOVE COPY AND STENCIL.

_____ 17. INFORM SUPERVISOR WHEN JOB IS COMPLETED.

WORKS AT STEADY PACE:

EXCESSIVE TALKING - NO. TIMES _____   TIME FINISHED_____

LEAVING WORK AREA - NO. TIMES _____   TIME STARTED_____

IDLE - NUMBER TIMES _____   TOTAL TIME_____

CODE   152

TOKENS _____

PERCENTAGE _____%

CENTER FOR DEVELOPMENTAL AND LEARNING DISORDERS
TOKEN ECONOMY

10/21/71   NAME_____

                           DATE_____

WORK AREA_____

CLEANING STAINLESS STEEL

TOKEN VALUE 3

YES   NO

_____ 1. ASSEMBLE SUPPLIES:
              A. SPONGE
              B. ALL PURPOSE CLEANSER
              C. DIVIDED PLASTIC BUCKET—WATER IN ONE SIDE
              D. TWO OR THREE CLEAN RAGS

_____ 2. ITEMS TO BE POLISHED IN YOUR ASSIGNED AREA ARE:
              DOOR HANDLES (NOT KNOBS)
              DOOR HAND PLATES
              DOOR KICK PLATES
              ELEVATOR STAINLESS STEEL TRIM (INSIDE AND OUTSIDE)
              FIRE DOOR
              CRASH BARS
              BASE PLUGS
              SWITCH PLATES
              DOOR HINGES

_____ 3. DIP SPONGE INTO CLEANSER.

_____ 4. SCRUB ALL STAINLESS STEEL WITH SPONGE.

_____ 5. RINSE SPONGE IN CLEAN WATER FROM DIVIDED BUCKET AND
              RINSE OFF CLEANSER.

_____ 6. SPRAY ONE SQUIRT OF STAINLESS STEEL POLISH ON CLOTH AND
              APPLY TO STAINLESS STEEL.

_____ 7. BUFF TO HIGH SHINE WITH CLEAN, DRY RAG.

_____ 8. INFORM SUPERVISOR WHEN TASK IS COMPLETED.

WORKS AT STEADY PACE:

EXCESSIVE TALKING - NO. TIMES _____   TIME FINISHED_____

LEAVING WORK AREA - NO. TIMES _____   TIME STARTED_____

IDLE - NUMBER TIMES _____   TOTAL TIME_____

                    CODE 137

                    TOKENS _____

                    PERCENTAGE _____%

CENTER FOR DEVELOPMENTAL AND LEARNING DISORDERS
TOKEN ECONOMY

10/22/71   NAME_____

                            DATE_____

CLEANING OF REFRIGERATOR

TOKEN VALUE 3

YES   NO

_____ 1. ASSEMBLE SUPPLIES AND EQUIPMENT:
               CLOTHS   TRAYS
               BOWL OR PAN   BAKING SODA
_____ 2. FILL BOWL HALF FULL OF WARM WATER. PUT 2 TABLESPOONS
               BAKING SODA IN WATER AND MIX TILL DISSOLVED.
_____ 3. TAKE FOODS FROM REFRIGERATOR AND PUT ON TRAYS.
_____ 4. DAMPEN A CLOTH IN THE WARM WATER AND WIPE OUT INSIDE
               OF REFRIGERATOR STARTING AT THE TOP.
_____ 5. RINSE CLOTH OUT IN WATER OFTEN.
_____ 6. WIPE OFF SHELVES CAREFULLY.
_____ 7. WIPE OFF INSIDE OF DOOR AND TRAYS OF DOOR CAREFULLY.
_____ 8. WHEN REFRIGERATOR IS WIPED OUT COMPLETELY, PUT CLEAN,
               WARM RINSE WATER IN BOWL.
_____ 9. GO OVER INSIDE OF REFRIGERATOR WITH CLEAN CLOTH RINSED
               IN CLEAN WATER IN BOWL.
_____ 10. WHEN REFRIGERATOR IS COMPLETELY RINSED, TAKE DRY CLOTH
               AND DRY OUT INSIDE OF REFRIGERATOR.
_____ 11. CHECK EACH CONTAINER GETTING RID OF ANY OLD OR
               UNUSABLE FOODS.
_____ 12. TAKE THE CLOTH USED FOR RINSING AND WIPE OFF REMAINING
               CONTAINERS ON THE TRAYS.
_____ 13. DRY TRAYS WITH THE DRYING CLOTH USED FOR DRYING
               REFRIGERATOR.
_____ 14. PUT CONTAINERS AND FOOD PACKAGES BACK INTO
               REFRIGERATOR.
_____ 15. WASH AND DRY BOWLS, TRAYS AND EMPTIED FOOD CONTAINERS.
_____ 16. PUT AWAY ALL SUPPLIES AND EQUIPMENT.
_____ 17. LEAVE WORK AREA CLEAN (SINK AND COUNTERS).
_____ 18. PUT USED CLOTHS IN LAUNDRY.
_____ 19. INFORM SUPERVISOR WHEN WORK IS FINISHED.

WORKS AT STEADY PACE:

EXCESSIVE TALKING - NO. TIMES _____   TIME FINISHED_____

LEAVING WORK AREA - NO. TIMES _____   TIME STARTED_____

IDLE - NUMBER TIMES _____   TOTAL TIME_____

                            CODE 025

                            TOKENS _____

                            PERCENTAGE_____%

CENTER FOR DEVELOPMENTAL AND LEARNING DISORDERS
TOKEN ECONOMY

10/22/71   NAME_____

WORK AREA_____ DATE_____

VACUUMING CARPET

TOKEN VALUE 2

YES   NO

_____ 1. ASSEMBLE SUPPLIES:
          A. UPRIGHT VACUUM CLEANER   B. DUST CLOTH

_____ 2. ROLL VACUUM TO AREA TO BE CLEANED STAYING ON THE RIGHT SIDE OF THE HALL.

_____ 3. PLUG CORD INTO THE ELECTRICAL OUTLET NEAREST THE CARPET TO BE VACUUMED.

_____ 4. START VACUUMING THE SIDES OF THE CARPET AND MOVE TO THE CENTER OF THE CARPET USING SLOW, SHORT PUSH-PULL STROKES. MOVE LIGHT OBJECTS SUCH AS TRASH BASKETS, FLOOR LAMPS, ETC.

_____ 5. VACUUM ENTIRE CARPET IN THIS MANNER; CLEAN UNDER DESKS, TABLES, COUCHES, ETC.

_____ 6. DO NOT SCAR OR SCUFF THE BASEBOARDS, FURNITURE, ETC. WITH THE VACUUM CLEANER.

_____ 7. MAKE SURE THE ENTIRE CARPET IS FREE OF ALL DUST PARTICLES AND OBJECTS.

_____ 8. REPLACE ALL ITEMS THAT YOU HAVE MOVED.

_____ 9. WIND CORD LOOSELY AROUND BRACKETS ON VACUUM; WIPE VACUUM CLEAN AND PLACE IN STORAGE AREA.

_____ 10. REPORT SPOTS AND STAINS TO YOUR SUPERVISOR.

WORKS AT STEADY PACE:

   EXCESSIVE TALKING - NO. TIMES _____   TIME FINISHED_____

   LEAVING WORK AREA - NO. TIMES _____   TIME STARTED_____

   IDLE - NUMBER TIMES _____   TOTAL TIME_____

CODE 134

TOKENS _____

PERCENTAGE _____%

CENTER FOR DEVELOPMENTAL AND LEARNING DISORDERS
TOKEN ECONOMY

10/13/72

NAME_____

DATE_____

JIGSAW OPERATION

TOKEN VALUE 3 per ½ hour

YES   NO

_____ 1. SET UPPER SUPPORT ARM FOR PROPER PRESSURE ON WOOD TO BE CUT.

_____ 2. PROCEED TO CUT USING FIRM STEADY PRESSURE.

_____ 3. FOLLOW CUTTING LINE.

_____ 4. RETURN UNUSED MATERIAL TO DESIGNATED STORAGE AREA.

_____ 5. CLEAN UP SAW AREA.

_____ 6. INFORM SUPERVISOR WHEN FINISHED.

WORKS AT STEADY PACE:

EXCESSIVE TALKING - NO. TIMES _____   TIME FINISHED_____

LEAVING WORK AREA - NO. TIMES _____   TIME STARTED_____

IDLE - NUMBER TIMES _____   TOTAL TIME_____

CODE 085

TOKENS_____

PERCENTAGE_____ %

CENTER FOR DEVELOPMENTAL AND LEARNING DISORDERS
TOKEN ECONOMY

11/16/72   NAME_____

                                           DATE__ _ _____

BAND SAW OPERATION

TOKEN VALUE 3 per ½ hour

YES   NO

_____ 1. SET UPPER SUPPORT ARM FOR PROPER WOOD CLEARANCE.

_____ 2. PROCEED TO CUT USING FIRM STEADY PRESSURE.

_____ 3. FOLLOW CUTTING LINE.

_____ 4. WHEN FINISHED, STOP MACHINE.

_____ 5. CLEAN WORK AREA.

_____ 6. INFORM SUPERVISOR WHEN FINISHED.

WORKS AT STEADY PACE:

EXCESSIVE TALKING - NO. TIMES _____   TIME FINISHED_____

LEAVING WORK AREA - NO. TIMES _____   TIME STARTED_____

IDLE - NUMBER TIMES _____   TOTAL TIME_____

CODE   070

TOKENS _____

PERCENTAGE _____%

CENTER FOR DEVELOPMENTAL AND LEARNING DISORDERS
TOKEN ECONOMY

2/15/72

AREAS_____   NAME_____

_____   ·DATE_____

VACUUMING ADL

ITEMS TO BE VACUUMED: TOKEN VALUE 3 per ½ hour

YES   NO
_____
             1. _____
             2. _____

_____   1. ASSEMBLE NECESSARY EQUIPMENT:
                 A. VACUUM CLEANER
                 B. ATTACHMENTS FOR VACUUM CLEANER

_____   2. PLUG VACUUM CLEANER INTO WALL SOCKET NEAR AREA TO BE
                 VACUUMED.

_____   3. ATTACH CORRECT BRUSH FOR JOB TO BE DONE WITH THE
                 VACUUM CLEANER.

_____   4. TURN ON VACUUM CLEANER.

_____   5. MOVE ATTACHMENT BACK AND FORTH OVER ENTIRE AREA TO
                 BE VACUUMED. USE SHORT STROKES.

_____   6. TURN OFF VACUUM CLEANER WHEN FINISHED.

_____   7. UNPLUG VACUUM CLEANER AND PUT IN PROPER PLACE WITH
                 ALL ITS ATTACHMENTS.

_____   8. REPORT TO SUPERVISOR WHEN TASK IS COMPLETED.

WORKS AT STEADY PACE:

   EXCESSIVE TALKING - NO. TIMES _____   TIME FINISHED_____

   LEAVING WORK AREA - NO. TIMES _____   TIME STARTED_____

   IDLE - NUMBER TIMES _____   TOTAL TIME_____

CODE   036

TOKENS _____

PERCENTAGE _____%

CENTER FOR DEVELOPMENTAL AND LEARNING DISORDERS
TOKEN ECONOMY

10/2/72   NAME_____

                                 DATE_____

CLEANING STOVE

TOKEN VALUE 3 per ½ hour

YES   NO

_____   1. ASSEMBLE SUPPLIES AND EQUIPMENT:
                 A. SINK FULL OF HOT, SOAPY WATER   C. ALUMINUM FOIL
                 B. CLOTHS   D. POLISH
_____   2. RAISE STOVE EYES AND REMOVE RIMS AND DRIP PANS.
_____   3. REMOVE FOIL COVERING ON DRIP PANS AND DISCARD.
_____   4. WASH AND CLEAN AND RINSE DRIP PANS UNTIL FREE OF DIRT,
                 GRIT, GRIME, BAKED-ON FOOD. DRY CAREFULLY.
_____   5. WIPE OUT UNDER STOVE EYES AND RIMS OF STOVE EYES
                 REMOVING ALL GRIME, GREASE AND DIRT.
_____   6. TEAR OFF PIECES OF FOIL TO LINE DRIP PANS LEAVING CENTER
                 FREE AND MOLDING FOIL AROUND NOTCH IN PAN.
_____   7. REPLACE COVERED DRIP PANS IN EYES, PLACING NOTCHES AT
                 REAR OF STOVE EYE.
_____   8. REPLACE RIMS ON STOVE EYES PLACING SEAM OF RIM AT BACK
                 OF EYE.
_____   9. LOWER STOVE COILS.
_____   10. CLEAN ENTIRE SURFACE OF STOVE WIPING OFF ALL DUST, DIRT,
                 GREASE AND GRIME WITH SOAPY WATER.
_____   11. RINSE STOVE REMOVING ALL TRACES OF SOAP SUDS.
_____   12. DRY STOVE RUBBING UNTIL NO WATER STREAKS OR SPOTS ARE
                 LEFT.
_____   13. POLISH ENTIRE SURFACE OF STOVE REMOVING ANY TRACES OF
                 STREAKS OR PRINTS RUBBING UNTIL STOVE HAS SHINY SMOOTH
                 SURFACE.
_____   14. REPLACE ANY SUPPLIES USED.
_____   15. CLEAN SINK.
_____   16. PUT CLOTHS USED IN LAUNDRY BUCKET.
_____   17. LEAVE WORK AREA AND LAUNDRY BUCKET CLEAN AND IN ORDER.
_____   18. INFORM SUPERVISOR WHEN WORK IS COMPLETED.

WORKS AT STEADY PACE:

EXCESSIVE TALKING - NO. TIMES_____   TIME FINISHED_____

LEAVING WORK AREA - NO. TIMES_____   TIME STARTED_____

IDLE - NUMBER TIMES_____   TOTAL TIME_____

CODE 159

TOKENS_____

PERCENTAGE_____%

CENTER FOR DEVELOPMENTAL AND LEARNING DISORDERS
TOKEN ECONOMY

10/22/71

NAME_____

DATE_____

DUPLICATING MACHINE OPERATOR

TOKEN VALUE 3 per ½ hour

YES   NO
_____

_____ 1. READ REQUEST FORM TO DETERMINE NUMBER OF COPIES.

_____ 2. REMOVE PROTECTIVE COVER FROM CYLINDER; ATTACH STENCIL TO CYLINDER. USE SCRAP PAPER TO RUN FIRST 5 TO 10 COPIES.

_____ 3. CHECK INK LEVEL IF COPIES ON SCRAP PAPER ARE NOT CLEAR. LOAD PAPER ON FEED TABLE. (ADJUST RAILS IF NECESSARY.)

_____ 4. RUN APPROPRIATE NUMBER OF COPIES.

_____ 5. REMOVE STENCIL FROM CYLINDER AND ATTACH PROTECTIVE COVER TO CYLINDER.

_____ 6. STAND WHILE OPERATING MACHINE.

_____ 7. WATCH MACHINE CONSTANTLY.

_____ 8. CLEAN MACHINE AND WORK AREA.

_____ 9. REPLACE MACHINE COVER AFTER USE.

_____ 10. RETURN ALL SUPPLIES TO CABINET.

_____ 11. DELIVER COMPLETED COPIES TO DESIGNATED ROOM ON REQUEST FORM. RETURN IMMEDIATELY.

_____ 12. INFORM SUPERVISOR WHEN JOB IS COMPLETED.

WORKS AT STEADY PACE:

EXCESSIVE TALKING - NO. TIMES _____   TIME FINISHED_____

LEAVING WORK AREA - NO. TIMES _____   TIME STARTED_____

IDLE - NUMBER TIMES _____   TOTAL TIME_____

CODE 076

TOKENS _____

PERCENTAGE _____%

**CENTER FOR DEVELOPMENTAL AND LEARNING DISORDERS
TOKEN ECONOMY**

11/20/72   NAME_____

                            DATE_____

SETTING UP COFFEE TRAY

TOKEN VALUE 3 per ½ hour

YES   NO

_____ 1. ASSEMBLE EQUIPMENT AND MATERIAL:
                CLOTH TO COVER TRAY   TRAY   SUGAR
                INSTANT COFFEE   CUPS   NAPKINS
                COFFEE POT   CREAM   SPOONS
_____ 2. FILL CREAM, SUGAR AND COFFEE POT IF NEEDED.
_____ 3. FILL POT WITH WATER.
_____ 4. ARRANGE CUPS, NAPKINS, SPOONS, COFFEE, CREAM AND SUGAR ON
                TRAY WITH CLOTH.
_____ 5. TAKE TRAY AND COFFEE POT TO DESIGNATED PLACE.
_____ 6. PUT AWAY EQUIPMENT AND MATERIALS WHEN FINISHED.
_____ 7. INFORM SUPERVISOR WHEN FINISHED.

WORKS AT STEADY PACE:

EXCESSIVE TALKING - NO. TIMES _____   TIME FINISHED_____

LEAVING WORK AREA - NO. TIMES _____   TIME STARTED_____

IDLE - NUMBER TIMES _____   TOTAL TIME_____

CODE 049

TOKENS _____

PERCENTAGE _____%

CENTER FOR DEVELOPMENTAL AND LEARNING DISORDERS
TOKEN ECONOMY

3/28/72

NAME_____

DATE_____

DRILL PRESS OPERATOR

TOKEN VALUE 3 per ½ hour

YES   NO

_____ 1. SET DRILL PRESS FOR PROPER CLEARANCE.

_____ 2. PROCEED TO DRILL USING FIRM STEADY PRESSURE.

_____ 3. FOLLOW PATTERN OUTLINE.

_____ 4. WHEN FINISHED, STOP MACHINE.

_____ 5. CLEAN DRILL PRESS WORK AREA.

_____ 6. INFORM SUPERVISOR WHEN FINISHED.

WORKS AT STEADY PACE:

EXCESSIVE TALKING - NO. TIMES _____   TIME FINISHED_____

LEAVING WORK AREA - NO. TIMES _____   TIME STARTED_____

IDLE - NUMBER TIMES _____   TOTAL TIME_____

CODE 075

TOKENS _____

PERCENTAGE _____%

CENTER FOR DEVELOPMENTAL AND LEARNING DISORDERS
TOKEN ECONOMY

10/13/72

NAME_____ _____

DATE_____

HAND BELT SANDER OPERATION

TOKEN VALUE 3 per ½ hour

YES   NO

_____ 1. MAKE CERTAIN PROPER GRIT IS ON MACHINE.

_____ 2. PLACE MATERIAL IN FIXED POSITION ON WORK TABLE.

_____ 3. PUSH SANDER ACROSS OBJECT USING AN EVEN SMOOTH MOTION.

_____ 4. CLEAN SANDER AND STORE IN DESIGNATED PLACE.

_____ 5. PLACE MATERIAL IN DESIGNATED STORAGE PLACE.

_____ 6. INFORM SUPERVISOR WHEN TASK IS COMPLETED.

WORKS AT STEADY PACE:

EXCESSIVE TALKING - NO. TIMES_____   TIME FINISHED_____

LEAVING WORK AREA - NO. TIMES_____   TIME STARTED_____

IDLE - NUMBER TIMES_____   TOTAL TIME_____

CODE 071

TOKENS_____

PERCENTAGE_____%

CENTER FOR DEVELOPMENTAL AND LEARNING DISORDERS
TOKEN ECONOMY

2/15/72   NAME_____

DATE_____

FOLDING TOWELS

TOKEN VALUE 2

YES   NO

_____   1. GATHER BATH TOWELS, DISH TOWELS, HAND TOWELS, WASH
CLOTHS ON THE TABLE IN LAUNDRY ROOM.

_____   2. TAKE ALL TOWELS AND CLOTHS TO WORK AREA.

_____   3. FOLD TOWELS LENGTHWISE ONCE THEN CROSSWISE ONCE.

_____   4. PLACE FOLDED TOWELS IN STORAGE PLACE.

_____   5. INFORM SUPERVISOR WHEN TASK IS COMPLETED.

TIME FINISHED_____

TIME STARTED_____

TOTAL TIME_____

CODE 030

TOKENS _____

PERCENTAGE _____%

CENTER FOR DEVELOPMENTAL AND LEARNING DISORDERS
TOKEN ECONOMY

10/20/71   NAME_____

                           DATE_____

IRONING

TOKEN VALUE 3 per ½ hour

YES   NO

_____ 1. ASSEMBLE EQUIPMENT AND BEGIN IRONING WITHIN 10 MINUTES.
                        A. IRON
                        B. SPRAY STARCH OR SIZING
                        C. GARMENTS TO BE IRONED
                        D. IRONING BOARD
                        E. SMALL PITCHER OF WATER
                        F. GARMENT HANGERS

_____ 2. PUT IRONING BOARD UP IN WORK AREA THAT IS WELL-LIGHTED.

_____ 3. FILL IRON WITH WATER.

_____ 4. PLUG IRON INTO SOCKET.

_____ 5. SET IRON AT TEMPERATURE FOR GARMENT OR MATERIAL THAT IS TO BE IRONED.

_____ 6. AFTER IRON IS HEATED, SPRAY AN AREA OF THE GARMENT NO LARGER THAN A HAND WITH STARCH OR SIZING AND MOVE IRON BACK AND FORTH SLOWLY MAKING SURE TO SMOOTH OUT ALL WRINKLES.

_____ 7. CONTINUE TO PERFORM STEP 6 UNTIL ENTIRE GARMENT IS IRONED.

_____ 8. FOLD GARMENT OR PLACE ON HANGER AND TAKE IT TO THE AREA TO WHICH IT BELONGS.

_____ 9. TURN OFF AND UNPLUG IRON.

_____ 10. EMPTY EXCESS WATER FROM IRON INTO SINK.

_____ 11. LEAVE IRON IN UPRIGHT POSITION WITH CORD CURLED BESIDE IRON.

_____ 12. RETURN EQUIPMENT TO CABINETS.

_____ 13. CLEAN WORK AREA.

_____ 14. CHECK WITH SUPERVISOR WHEN TASK IS COMPLETED.

WORKS AT STEADY PACE:

EXCESSIVE TALKING - NO. TIMES _____   TIME FINISHED_____

LEAVING WORK AREA - NO. TIMES _____   TIME STARTED_____

IDLE - NUMBER TIMES _____   TOTAL TIME_____

CODE 046

TOKENS _____

PERCENTAGE _____%

CENTER FOR DEVELOPMENTAL AND LEARNING DISORDERS
TOKEN ECONOMY

NAME_____

WORK AREA_____ DATE_____

CLEANING STAIRWELL HANDRAILS

TOKEN VALUE 2

YES   NO

_____ 1. ASSEMBLE MATERIALS:
ONE PLASTIC BUCKET ½ FULL OF CLEAN WATER
ONE SCRUB BACKED SPONGE
FOUR CLEAN RAGS
ALL-PURPOSE CLEANER
STAINLESS STEEL POLISH

_____ 2. PROCEED TO WORK AREA. PLACE SUPPLIES IN CORNER OF STAIRWELL.

_____ 3. WITH DAMP CLOTH, APPLY CLEANER TO HANDRAILS WORKING DOWN THE STAIRS TO THE NEXT LANDING.

_____ 4. WORKING UP THE STAIRS, SCRUB RAIL WITH SPONGE.

_____ 5. WORKING DOWN THE STAIRS, WIPE OFF ALL CLEANER AND GRIME WITH CLEAN, DAMP RAG.

_____ 6. WORKING UP THE STAIRS, DRY RAIL WITH CLEAN, DRY RAG.

_____ 7. WORKING DOWN THE STAIRS, APPLY ONE SQUIRT OF STAINLESS STEEL POLISH TO CLEAN RAG AND WORK INTO RAIL.

_____ 8. WORKING UP THE STAIRS, BUFF TO HIGH SHINE WITH 4th CLEAN RAG.

_____ 9. CLEAN AND DRY STORE EQUIPMENT AND SUPPLIES.

_____ 10. INFORM SUPERVISOR WHEN JOB IS FINISHED.

WORKS AT STEADY PACE:

EXCESSIVE TALKING - NO. TIMES _____   TIME FINISHED_____

LEAVING WORK AREA - NO. TIMES _____   TIME STARTED_____

IDLE - NUMBER TIMES _____   TOTAL TIME_____

CODE 123

TOKENS _____

PERCENTAGE _____ %

CENTER FOR DEVELOPMENTAL AND LEARNING DISORDERS
TOKEN ECONOMY

10/21/71   NAME_____

WORK AREA_____ DATE_____

CARE OF CIGARETTE URNS

TOKEN VALUE 2

YES   NO

_____ 1. ASSEMBLE SUPPLIES AND EQUIPMENT:
              A. TWO PLASTIC BUCKETS ½ FULL OF CLEAN WATER
              B. TWO SPONGES
              C. TWO OR THREE CLEAN, DRY RAGS
              D. ONE CAN STAINLESS STEEL POLISH
              E. CLEANSER
              F. PLASTIC BAG
_____ 2. PROCEED TO WORK AREA.
_____ 3. REMOVE TOP OF CIGARETTE URN AND INNER LINER. PLACE IN
              WATER TO SOAK. PLACE ANY TRASH AND CIGARETTES IN THE
              PLASTIC TRASH BAG.
_____ 4. USE DAMP SPONGE AND CLEANSER TO CLEAN ENTIRE INSIDE AND
              OUTSIDE OF URN.
_____ 5. RINSE URN WITH FRESH WATER FROM SECOND BUCKET OF
              WATER.
_____ 6. DRY URN.
_____ 7. DRY AND REPLACE INNER LINER.
_____ 8. ADD ENOUGH WATER SO THAT 2 INCHES OF WATER IS LEFT IN
              THE URN.
_____ 9. WIPE TO A SHINE AND DRY THE TOP. REPLACE THE TOP.
_____ 10. COAT OUTSIDE OF URN WITH STAINLESS STEEL POLISH.
_____ 11. BUFF WITH A DRY RAG.
_____ 12. INFORM SUPERVISOR WHEN JOB IS COMPLETED.

WORKS AT STEADY PACE:

EXCESSIVE TALKING - NO. TIMES _____   TIME FINISHED_____

LEAVING WORK AREA - NO. TIMES _____   TIME STARTED_____

IDLE - NUMBER TIMES _____   TOTAL TIME_____

CODE 120

TOKENS _____

PERCENTAGE _____ %

APPENDIX C

EXAMPLES OF
RED LEVEL JOB DESCRIPTIONS

CENTER FOR DEVELOPMENTAL AND LEARNING DISORDERS
TOKEN ECONOMY

9/25/72

NAME_____

DATE_____

SIGN MAKING

TOKEN VALUE 3 per ½ hour

YES   NO

_____ 1. READ REQUEST FORM FOR SIGN.

_____ 2. SELECT PROPER LETTERS FOR SIGN.

_____ 3. LAY OUT LETTERING ON SIGN PROPERLY SPACED.

_____ 4. HAVE LAYOUT CHECKED BY SUPERVISOR.

_____ 5. WET LETTERS WITH SPONGE AND APPLY TO CARDBOARD WITHIN DRAWN BORDERS.

_____ 6. INFORM SUPERVISOR WHEN SIGN IS COMPLETED.

WORKS AT STEADY PACE:

EXCESSIVE TALKING - NO. TIMES _____   TIME FINISHED_____

LEAVING WORK AREA - NO. TIMES _____   TIME STARTED_____

IDLE - NUMBER TIMES _____   TOTAL TIME_____

CODÉ 146

TOKENS _____

PERCENTAGE _____ %

CENTER FOR DEVELOPMENTAL AND LEARNING DISORDERS
TOKEN ECONOMY

11/15/72   NAME_____

AREA_____   DATE_____

BUFFING MACHINE OPERATOR

TOKEN VALUE 3 per ½ hour

YES   NO

_____   1. ASSEMBLE MATERIALS:

      A. DUST MOP AND COVER   F. COUNTER BRUSH & DUSTPAN
      B. POLISHING BRUSH OR PAD   G. MOP DOLLY
      C. BUFFING MACHINE   H. TWO OVAL BUCKETS
      D. STEEL WOOL PAD   I. TWO 24-OUNCE MOPS
      E. CLEANING SOLUTION   J. "WET FLOOR" SIGNS

_____   2. PROCEED TO WORK AREA TRAVELING ON THE RIGHT SIDE OF THE HALL.

_____   3. DUST MOP ENTIRE AREA TO BE BUFFED.

_____   4. SET UP "WET FLOOR" SIGNS.

_____   5. MOISTEN STEEL WOOL PAD IN CLEANING SOLUTION AND SCRUB SCUFF MARKS BY HAND OR USING PAD UNDER YOUR FOOT.

_____   6. WET MOP ENTIRE AREA.

_____   7. BUFF ENTIRE AREA.

_____   8. DUST MOP ENTIRE AREA IMMEDIATELY AFTER BUFFING.

_____   9. PICK UP DUST WITH DUSTPAN AND COUNTER BRUSH.

_____   10. RETURN ALL EQUIPMENT TO STORAGE AREA.

_____   11. WASH AND DRY BUCKETS AND DUSTPAN AND STORE.

_____   12. WASH AND DRY DOLLY.

_____   13. DRY WIPE ENTIRE BUFFER BASE. DAMP WIPE BUFFER CORD.

_____   14. STORE BUFFER ON ITS BACK.

_____   15. SHAKE OUT DUST MOP AND HANG UP BY HANDLE.

_____   16. INFORM SUPERVISOR WHEN TASK IS COMPLETED.

WORKS AT STEADY PACE:

EXCESSIVE TALKING - NO. TIMES _____   TIME FINISHED_____

LEAVING WORK AREA - NO. TIMES _____   TIME STARTED_____

IDLE - NUMBER TIMES _____   TOTAL TIME_____

CODE   127

TOKENS _____

PERCENTAGE _____ %

CENTER FOR DEVELOPMENTAL AND LEARNING DISORDERS
TOKEN ECONOMY

NAME_____

DATE_____

PHOTOCOPY MACHINE OPERATOR

TOKEN VALUE 3 per ½ hour

YES   NO

_____ 1. SEE INSTRUCTOR FOR MATERIAL TO BE COPIED.

_____ 2. MAKE SURE NUMBER OF COPIES TO BE MADE IS ON EACH PIECE OF PAPER.

_____ 3. GO TO ASSIGNED MACHINE.

_____ 4. TURN DIAL TO INDICATE NUMBER OF COPIES TO BE MADE.

_____ 5. INSERT PAPER TO BE COPIED INTO MACHINE.

_____ 6. PUSH "START" BUTTON TO MAKE COPIES.

_____ 7. WHEN MACHINE IS FINISHED COPYING, REMOVE ORIGINAL COPY FROM MACHINE.

_____ 8. FOLLOW STEPS 4, 5, 6 AND 7 FOR OTHER COPIES.

_____ 9. RECORD NUMBER OF USABLE COPIES AND UNUSABLE COPIES IN THE RECORD BOOK.

_____ 10. RETURN TO INSTRUCTOR ALL NEW COPIES MADE AS WELL AS ORIGINAL COPIES.

WORKS AT STEADY PACE:

EXCESSIVE TALKING - NO. TIMES _____   TIME FINISHED_____

LEAVING WORK AREA - NO. TIMES _____   TIME STARTED_____

IDLE - NUMBER TIMES _____   TOTAL TIME_____

CODE   193

TOKENS_____

PERCENTAGE_____ %

CENTER FOR DEVELOPMENTAL AND LEARNING DISORDERS
TOKEN ECONOMY

NAME_____

DATE_____

WORK REQUEST

TOKEN VALUE_____

DESCRIPTION:

TIME FINISHED_____

TIME STARTED_____

TOTAL TIME_____

CODE 116

TOKENS_____

PERCENTAGE_____%

CENTER FOR DEVELOPMENTAL AND LEARNING DISORDERS
TOKEN ECONOMY

NAME_____

DATE_____

BUS DRIVER (MORNING)

TOKEN VALUE 8

YES   NO

_____ 1. PICK UP STUDENTS AT PICK-UP POINTS.
_____ 2. PUT STUDENTS IN SEATS AND SEE THAT SEAT BELTS ARE
               BUCKLED.
_____ 3. DRIVE STUDENTS SAFELY TO CDLD.
_____ 4. SEE THAT STUDENTS GET TO RIGHT CLASSROOMS.
_____ 5. RETURN KEY TO ROOM 521 AND REPORT ANY DIFFICULTY WHICH
               YOU MAY HAVE HAD.

TIME FINISHED_____

TIME STARTED_____

TOTAL TIME_____

CODE 183

TOKENS_____

PERCENTAGE_____%

CENTER FOR DEVELOPMENTAL AND LEARNING DISORDERS
TOKEN ECONOMY

NAME_____

DATE_____

BUS DRIVER (AFTERNOON)

TOKEN VALUE 8

YES   NO

_____ 1. GET STUDENTS FROM CLASSES.

_____ 2. PUT STUDENTS IN SEATS AND SEE THAT SEAT BELTS ARE
BUCKLED.

_____ 3. DRIVE STUDENTS SAFELY HOME.

_____ 4. RETURN DIRECTLY TO CDLD.

_____ 5. RETURN KEY TO ROOM 521 AND REPORT ANY DIFFICULTY WHICH
YOU MAY HAVE HAD.

TIME FINISHED_____

TIME STARTED_____

TOTAL TIME_____

CODE 183

TOKENS _____

PERCENTAGE _____%

CENTER FOR DEVELOPMENTAL AND LEARNING DISORDERS
TOKEN ECONOMY

10/13/72   NAME_____

DATE_____

MAIL CLERK

TOKEN VALUE 4

TIME 30-45 MINUTES

YES   NO

_____ 1. REPORT TO 1ST FLOOR MAIL BOXES AT 10:30 A.M. AND 2:00 P.M.

_____ 2. SORT MAIL DEPOSITED IN TRAY.
               A. SORT CAMPUS MAIL
               B. SORT MAIL WITH POSTAGE STAMPS
               C. SORT MAIL BY GRANT NUMBERS
               D. COLLECT MAIL NOT FOR CDLD
               E. PLACE RUBBER BANDS AROUND SORTED MAIL

_____ 3. PLACE SORTED MAIL INTO MAIL BASKET.

_____ 4. PLACE MAIL WITH STAMPS IN OUTGOING SLOT AT POST OFFICE.

_____ 5. GO TO THE MAIL BOX AT BASIC SCIENCES BUILDING.

_____ 6. PLACE CAMPUS MAIL INTO CAMPUS MAIL SLOT.

_____ 7. DEPOSIT OUTGOING MAIL AT POST OFFICE COUNTER.

_____ 8. UNLOCK MAIL BOXES NOS. 311 & 313 BY COMBINATION.

_____ 9. COLLECT MAIL FROM BOXES AND PLACE INTO BASKET.

_____ 10. RETURN TO CDLD.

_____ 11. SORT ALL MAIL INTO MAIL BOXES ON 1ST FLOOR.

_____ 12. INFORM SUPERVISOR WHEN JOB IS FINISHED.

TIME FINISHED_____

TIME STARTED_____

TOTAL TIME_____

CODE 185

TOKENS _____

PERCENTAGE _____%

APPENDIX D

EXAMPLES OF
AUXILIARY WORK AND ACADEMIC JOB DESCRIPTIONS

CENTER FOR DEVELOPMENTAL AND LEARNING DISORDERS
TOKEN ECONOMY

2/9/72

NAME_____

DATE_____

GROOMING

TOKEN VALUE 4

YES   NO

_____ 1. CLEAN HAIR
>   A. NO OBVIOUS DANDRUFF
>   B. NON-GREASY (GIRLS)
>   C. NO EXCESSIVE HAIR TONIC (BOYS)

_____ 2. HAIR NEATLY COMBED

_____ 3. BODY CLEANLINESS
>   A. CLEAN TEETH
>   B. CLEAN ARMS (NO OBVIOUS MATERIAL)
>   C. CLEAN HANDS AND REASONABLE NEAT AND CLEAN
>   FINGERNAILS

_____ 4. NO BODY ODOR

_____ 5. CLEAN AND NEATLY PRESSED CLOTHES (NO OBVIOUS DIRT OR
EXCESSIVE WRINKLES)

_____ 6. CLEAN SHOES (FREE OF DIRT OR DUST—NOT OBVIOUSLY DIRTY)

_____ 7. CLEAN SHAVEN (BOYS)
SHAVEN LEGS AND UNDERARMS (ALL VISIBLE HAIR ON LEGS
SHOULD BE REMOVED—GIRLS)

_____ 8. NATURAL LOOKING AND NEATLY APPLIED MAKE-UP (GIRLS)
SOCKS (BOYS)

CODE 003

TOKENS _____

PERCENTAGE _____%

CENTER FOR DEVELOPMENTAL AND LEARNING DISORDERS
TOKEN ECONOMY

9/8/71   NAME_____

                          DATE_____

RESOURCE ROOM

DUKANE®—AVID® RECORDS

TOKEN VALUE 1 - 5

TIME   30 MINUTES

YES   NO

_____ 1. 0 - 30% - 1 TOKEN   _____

_____ 2. 31 - 70% - 2 TOKENS   CODE 014

_____ 3. 71 - 80% - 3 TOKENS   TOKENS_____

_____ 4. 81 - 90% - 4 TOKENS   PERCENTAGE_____%

_____ 5. 91 - 100% - 5 TOKENS   _____

HOFFMAN®

TOKEN VALUE 1 - 5

TIME   30 MINUTES

YES   NO

_____ 1. 0 - 30% - 1 TOKEN   _____

_____ 2. 31 - 70% - 2 TOKENS   CODE 016

_____ 3. 71 - 80% - 3 TOKENS   TOKENS_____

_____ 4. 81 - 90% - 4 TOKENS   PERCENTAGE_____%

_____ 5. 91 - 100% - 5 TOKENS   _____

AVIDESK®

TOKEN VALUE 1 - 5

YES   NO

_____ 1. 0 - 30% - 1 TOKEN   _____

_____ 2. 31 - 70% - 2 TOKENS   CODE 013

_____ 3. 71 - 80% - 3 TOKENS   TOKENS_____

_____ 4. 81 - 90% - 4 TOKENS   PERCENTAGE_____%

_____ 5. 91 - 100% - 5 TOKENS   _____

CENTER FOR DEVELOPMENTAL AND LEARNING DISORDERS
TOKEN ECONOMY

10/23/72

NAME_____

DATE_____

JUNIOR HIGH CLASS

READING

TOKEN VALUE 1 - 5

CODES 198 - 221

TIME 30 MINUTES

YES	NO
1 2 3 4 5 6 7	1 2 3 4 5 6 7

_____

_____

_____

_____

_____

1. 1-4 PAGES - 1 TOKEN

2.   5 PAGES - 2 TOKENS

3. 10 PAGES - 3 TOKENS

4. 15 PAGES - 4 TOKENS

5. 20 PAGES - 5 TOKENS

CODE ____

TOKENS_____

PERCENTAGE_____%

MATH

TOKEN VALUE 1 - 5

CODES 250 - 263

TIME 30 MINUTES

YES	NO
1 2 3 4 5 6 7	1 2 3 4 5 6 7

_____

_____

_____

_____

_____

1. 1-4 PROBLEMS - 1 TOKEN

2.   5 PROBLEMS - 2 TOKENS

3. 10 PROBLEMS - 3 TOKENS

4. 15 PROBLEMS - 4 TOKENS

5. 20 PROBLEMS - 5 TOKENS

CODE ____

TOKENS_____

PERCENTAGE_____%

CENTER FOR DEVELOPMENTAL AND LEARNING DISORDERS
TOKEN ECONOMY

1/21/72   NAME_____

                                             DATE_____
SENIOR HIGH SCHOOL
CURRENT EVENTS
TOKEN VALUE 2

YES   NO
_____ TWO (2) TOKENS FOR THREE (3) NEWSPAPER CLIPPINGS.

CODE 196

TOKENS _____

PERCENTAGE _____%

READING
TOKEN VALUE 1 - 5
CODES 198 - 221

TIME 30 MINUTES
        YES   NO
 1 2 3 4 5 6 7   1 2 3 4 5 6 7

                                        1. 1-4 PAGES - 1 TOKEN
                                        2. 5 PAGES - 2 TOKENS
                                        3. 10 PAGES - 3 TOKENS
                                        4. 15 PAGES - 4 TOKENS
                                        5. 20 PAGES - 5 TOKENS

CODE ____

TOKENS _____

PERCENTAGE _____%

MATH
TOKEN VALUE 1 - 5
CODES 250 - 263

TIME 30 MINUTES
        YES   NO
 1 2 3 4 5 6 7   1 2 3 4 5 6 7

                                        1. 1-4 PROBLEMS - 1 TOKEN
                                        2. 5 PROBLEMS - 2 TOKENS
                                        3. 10 PROBLEMS - 3 TOKENS
                                        4. 15 PROBLEMS - 4 TOKENS
                                        5. 20 PROBLEMS - 5 TOKENS

CODE ____

TOKENS _____

PERCENTAGE _____%

CENTER FOR DEVELOPMENTAL AND LEARNING DISORDERS
TOKEN ECONOMY

9/20/72   NAME_____

                                           DATE_____

DRIVER'S EDUCATION HANDBOOK

TOKEN VALUE 1 - 4

TIME 30 MINUTES

YES		NO	
1	2	1	2

_____ 1. 1-2 PAGES - 1 TOKEN   _____

_____ 2. 3-4 PAGES - 2 TOKENS   CODE 011

_____ 3. 5-6 PAGES - 3 TOKENS
                                           TOKENS_____
_____ 4. 7-8 PAGES - 4 TOKENS
                                           PERCENTAGE_____%

DRIVER'S EDUCATION WORKBOOK

TOKEN VALUE 1 - 4

TIME 30 MINUTES

YES		NO	
1	2	1	2

_____ 1. 1-2 PAGES - 1 TOKEN   _____

_____ 2. 3-4 PAGES - 2 TOKENS   CODE 012

_____ 3. 5-6 PAGES - 3 TOKENS
                                           TOKENS_____
_____ 4. 7-8 PAGES - 4 TOKENS
                                           PERCENTAGE_____%

DRIVER EDUCATION QUIZ

TOKEN VALUE 1 - 5

YES	NO

_____ 1. 0 - 30% - 1 TOKEN   _____

_____ 2. 31 - 70% - 2 TOKENS   CODE 197

_____ 3. 71 - 80% - 3 TOKENS
                                           TOKENS_____
_____ 4. 81 - 90% - 4 TOKENS
                                           PERCENTAGE_____%
_____ 5. 91 - 100% - 5 TOKENS

CENTER FOR DEVELOPMENTAL AND LEARNING DISORDERS
TOKEN ECONOMY

1/21/72

NAME_____

DATE_____

RESOURCE ROOM

READING

TOKEN VALUE 1 - 5

CODES 198 - 221

TIME   30 MINUTES
YES   NO
1 2 3 4 5 6 7   1 2 3 4 5 6 7
_____
_____
_____
_____
_____

1. 1-4 PAGES - 1 TOKEN

2. 5 PAGES - 2 TOKENS

3. 10 PAGES - 3 TOKENS

4. 15 PAGES - 4 TOKENS

5. 20 PAGES - 5 TOKENS

CODE ____

TOKENS _____

PERCENTAGE _____ %

MATH

TOKEN VALUE 1 - 5

CODES 250 - 263

TIME   30 MINUTES
YES   NO
1 2 3 4 5 6 7   1 2 3 4 5 6 7
_____
_____
_____
_____
_____

1. 1-4 PROBLEMS - 1 TOKEN

2. 5 PROBLEMS - 2 TOKENS

3. 10 PROBLEMS - 3 TOKENS

4. 15 PROBLEMS - 4 TOKENS

5. 20 PROBLEMS - 5 TOKENS

CODE ____

TOKENS _____

PERCENTAGE _____ %

APPENDIX E

SUGGESTED TRAINING MATERIALS *

Articles

Ayllon, T., and Michael, J.: The psychiatric nurse as a behavioral engineer. *J Exper Anal Behav,* 2:323, 1959.

Bandura, A.: Behavioral modification through modeling procedures. In Krasner, L., and Ullmann, L. P. (Eds.): *Case Studies in Behavior Modification.* New York, HR&W, 1965.

Bandura, A.: Psychotherapy as a learning process. *Psychol Bull, 58:*143, 1961.

Bensberg, G. J., Colwell, C. N., and Cassell, R. H.: Teaching the profoundly retarded self-help activities by behavior shaping techniques. *Am J Ment Defic, 69:*674, 1965.

Bricker, W.: Introduction to behavior modification. *Peabody Papers in Human Development.* Nashville, Peabody College for Teachers, Department of Psychology, 1968.

Bijou, S. W.: The mentally retarded child. *Psychol Today, 2:*46, 1968.

Burchard, J. D.: Systematic socialization: A programmed environment for the habilitation of antisocial retardates. *Psychol Rec, 17:*461, 1967.

Cantrell, R. P., Cantrell, Mary L., Huddleston, C. M., and Wooldridge, R. L.: Contingency contracting with school problems. *J Appl Behav Anal, 2:*215, 1969.

Costello, C. G.: Behaviour therapy: Criticisms and confusions. *Behav Res Ther, 1:*159, 1963.

Gist, J. W., and Welch, M. W.: The use of behavior modification in a cooperative special education and vocational rehabilitation program. In Sigleman, Carol K. (Ed.) : *Behavior Modification in Three Settings.* Lubbock, Texas Tech University, in Press.**

Grunbaum, A.: Causality and the science of human behavior. *Am Sci, 40:*665, 1952.

Kazdin, A. E., and Bootzin, R. R.: The token economy: An evaluative review. *J Appl Behav Anal, 5:*343, 1972.

Lent, J. R.: Mimosa cottage: Experiment in hope. *Psychol Today, 2:*51, 1968.

Meyerson, L., Kerr, N., and Michael, J.: Behavior modification in rehabilitation. In Bijou, S. W., and Baer, D. M. (Eds.) : *Child Development: Readings in Experimental Analysis.* New York, Appleton, 1967.

Premack, D.: Toward empirical behavior laws: I. Positive reinforcement. *Psychol Rev, 66:*219, 1959.

Rogers, C. R., and Skinner, B. F.: Some issues concerning the control of human behavior: A symposium. *Science, 124:*1057, 1956.

Zimmerman, E. H., and Zimmerman, J.: The alteration of behavior in a special classroom situation. *J Exper Anal Behav, 5:*59, 1962.

Books

Ayllon, T., and Azrin, N.: *The Token Economy: A Motivational System for Therapy and Rehabilitation.* New York, Appleton, 1968.

Baldwin, V. L., Fredericks, H. D., and Brodsky, G.: *Isn't It Time He Outgrew This? or A Training Program for Parents of Retarded Children.* Springfield, Thomas, 1973.

Blackham, G. J., and Silberman, A.: *Modification of Child Behavior.* Belmont, Wadsworth, 1971.

Bradfield, R. H.: *Behavior Modification: The Human Effort.* San Rafael, Dimensions, 1970.

Breyer, N. L., and Axelrod, S.: *Behavior Modification: An Annotated Bibliography of Selected Behavior Modification Studies.* Lawrence, H & H Enterprises, 1972.

Espich, J. E., and Williams, B.: *Developing Programmed Instructional Materials.* Belmont, Fearon, 1967.

Hall, R. V.: *Behavior Modification: Applications in School and Home.* Lawrence, H & H Enterprises, Inc., 1971.

Hall, R. V.: *Behavior Modification: Basic Principles.* Lawrence, H & H, 1971.
Hall, R. V.: *Behavior Modification: The Measurement of Behavior.* Lawrence, H & H, 1971.
Hamerlynck, L. A., and Clark, F. C.: *Behavior Modification for Exceptional Children and Youth.* (monograph no. 2). Alberta, Canada, University of Calgary, 1971.
Holland, J. G., and Skinner, B. F.: *The Analysis of Behavior.* New York, McGraw, 1961.
Krasner, L., and Ullmann, L. P.: *Research in Behavior Modification.* New York, HR&W, 1965.
Mager, R. F.: *Preparing Instructional Objectives.* Palo Alto, Fearon, 1962.
Neisworth, J. T., Smith, R. M.: *Modifying Retarded Behavior.* Atlanta, H-M, 1972.
Panyan, Marion C.: *Behavior Modification: New Ways to Teach New Skills.* Lawrence, H & H, 1972.
Schaefer, H. H., and Martin, P. L.: *Behavioral Therapy.* New York, McGraw, 1969.
Skinner, B. F.: *Behavior of an Organism.* New York, Appleton, 1938.
Skinner, B. F.: *Cumulative Record.* New York, Appleton, 1961.
Skinner, B. F.: *Science and Human Behavior.* New York, MacMillan, 1953.
Skinner, B. F.: *The Technology of Teaching.* New York, Appleton, 1968.
Ullmann, L. P., and Krasner, L.: *Case Studies in Behavior Modification.* New York, HR&W, 1965.
Valett, R. E.: *Modifying Children's Behavior—A Guide for Parents and Professionals.* Belmont, Fearon, 1969.
Wenrich, W. W.: *A Primer of Behavior Modification.* Belmont, Brooks-Cole, 1970.
Wheeler, A. H., and Fox, W. L.: *Behavior Modification: A Teacher's Guide to Writing Instructional Objectives.* Lawrence, H & H, 1972.

Films

Bensberg, G. J., and Colwell, C. N.: Teaching the mentally retarded—a positive approach. 16mm film. Southwest Texas Educational Television Council. Southern Regional Educational Board, Atlanta, Georgia, 1967.
Brown, D. G.: Selected films on behavior modification. U.S. Public Health Service, Mental Health Services, Region IV, Atlanta, Georgia, 1967.

Journals

Exceptional Children, Official Journal of the Council for Exceptional Children, Jefferson Plaza, Suite 900, 1411 S. Jefferson Davis Highway, Arlington, Virginia 22202.
Journal of Applied Behavior Analysis, Department of Human Development, University of Kansas, Lawrence, Kansas 66044.
Journal of Experimental Analysis of Behavior, Kay Dinsmoor JEAB, Department of Psychology, Indiana University, Bloomington, Indiana 47401.
Journal of Rehabilitation, Official Publication of the National Rehabilitation Association, 1522 K. St., N.W., Washington, D.C. 20005.
School Application of Learning Theory (SALT), Kalamazoo Valley Intermediate School District, Box 2025, Kalamazoo, Michigan 49003.
Vocational Evaluation and Work Adjustment Association Bulletin, Official Bulletin of the Vocational Evaluation and Work Adjustment Association—A Division of the National Rehabilitation Association, 1522 K St., N.W., Washington, D.C. 20005.

---

*This is only a partial list of available training materials and is placed here for emphasis. The list of references will also be helpful as training materials.

** This article available through a monograph series published by the Rehabilitation Research and Training Project, Texas Tech University, Lubbock, Texas.

AUTHOR INDEX

SUBJECT INDEX